Power Boating: The Great Ideas Book

by William Carpenter

How To Buy & Sell, Equip, Trailer, Operate, Maintain, Store, and Insure Your Power Boat Successfully!

First Edition

Gemini Marine Publications, San Antonio, Texas
Copyright © 1995 William S. Carpenter

Power Boating: The Great Ideas Book
by William Carpenter

Published by:

Gemini Marine Publications
Post Office Box 700255
San Antonio, Texas 78270-0255 U.S.A.

Publisher's Cataloging in Publication
(Prepared by Quality Books, Inc.)

Carpenter, William Spencer.
Power Boating—the great ideas book : how to buy & sell, equip, trailer, operate, maintain, store, and insure your power boat successfully! / by William Carpenter.—1st ed.
p. cm.
Includes bibliographical references and index
ISBN 1-883818-09-5
Preassigned LCCN: *94-78110*
1. Motorboats—Handbooks, manuals, etc. I. Title.

GV835.C37 1994

797.1'25
QBI94-2191

Brief Table of Contents

Table of Contents

Chapter 2
Equipping the Boat—For Comfort and Safety

Chapter Three
Trailering—Maneuver with Confidence 97

Chapter Four
Operating the Boat—You're the Skipper 119

List of Illustrations

Acknowledgements

Thanks are extended to US Marine for many of the boat photographs used in this book. Its boat manufacturing divisions include Bayliner, Maxum, and Robalo. US Marine is the largest builder of quality boats in the world. For information about their products, please write US Marine at P.O. Box 9029, Everett, WA 98206, or call (206) 435-5571.

The technical assistance provided by Captain Paul W. Eccleston, Professional Guide, Corpus Christi, Texas, and Randy Knodel and Larry Voges of Sunchaser Marine, Canyon Lake, Texas, was most helpful in the development of this book. I want to thank Mr. G. Tom Moore, III, United States Power Squadron, San Antonio, Texas, for excellent suggestions.

The comments and suggestions of Joan Borer were extremely helpful during the preparation of the final draft. Thanks are extended to my son, Bill Carpenter, III, for computer assistance. Appreciation for assistance over the past two years is extended to John and Laurie McDonald, Dave and Abby Dentry, Ed and Maryrose Barker, Kathleen Carpenter, Drew and Martha Birnbaum, Mary Jayne Waibel, Tristan Borer, Sid Moody, and Tyler Thomas. The proofreading skills of Brooke M. Borer were of great assistance during the initial preparation of this manuscript.

Special thanks to Ann Kaplan and Jennifer Knoblock for copy-editing.

Interior design and typesetting by Sandy Brown, San Antonio, Texas, (210) 520-3392.

Cover by Jim Lewis, Visual Edge Graphic Design, San Antonio, Texas.

This book is written in memory of my beloved wife, Jean, whose courage and bright spirit remain an inspiration to us all.

Introduction

> *The purpose of this book is to increase your boating pleasure and satisfaction. We give you solid facts that greatly enrich and expand your boating and trailering skills.*

You get important and interesting power boating ideas, tips, and techniques ready for immediate use. Your skills and enjoyment will rapidly develop with this unique information.

We took an entirely new and different approach in developing this easy-reading book. The boring and confusing marine theory found in many boating publications simply wouldn't do here.

Instead our research revealed that there are essentially seven basic power boating topics. These are **Buying and Selling, Equipping, Trailering, Operating, Maintaining, Storing,** and **Insuring** your boat. We give you seven chapters, each unique to one of these topics.

This fact-rich book will empower you to really improve your operating skills...save you considerable cash by showing how to avoid many boat, engine, and trailer maintenance problems...and save you even more cash with our insider secrets of buying and selling, equipping, storing, and insuring your boat.

As an important bonus, you will experience a rush of excitement and confidence as you realize that this is the boating knowledge you especially need and want.

The insights we give you here have been learned the hard way by boating experts over many years on many waterways and highways. There simply is no better teacher than this experience.

Our focus is mainly on recreational power boats of less than 26 feet in length that ride on trailers to and from fresh water lakes and rivers, and to and from coastal and near off-shore waters. This book is for everyone interested in this type of boating...be they Beginners or Old Hands.

Now let's get under way. Initially, you may wish to scan the Table of Contents, the Index, and the Appendix to get a general idea of what's here. Then just start at the beginning and go right through the whole book. Or just randomly flip through the pages. That choice is yours. But no matter how you approach it, we bet you'll soon find something that pays for this book many times over.

Before shoving off, let's clarify a couple of terms we use throughout the book. "Power boat rig," "trailer boat rig," and "rig" are your boat, engine, and the trailer they ride on. "Power boat" and "trailer boat" are used interchangeably, as are engine and motor.

Many other marine expressions, with their definitions, appear in these pages. You also get an excellent listing of basic boating terms in the fact-filled Appendix.

We sincerely invite your ideas, suggestions, or any other comments about power boating or this book. Those things that seem so obvious to you in your boating experiences could well be a lifesaver to someone else. Please send these to Gemini Marine Publications, Post Office Box 700255, San Antonio, TX 78270-0255. Those we use will appear with appropriate full credit in future editions of this book, or in related publications.

Happy Boating!

Believe me, my young friend, there is nothing—absolutely nothing—half so much worth doing as simply messing about in boats.

Kenneth Grahame, *The Wind in the Willows*

Disclaimer

The purpose of this book is to educate and entertain. While every reasonable precaution has been taken in the preparation of this publication, the author and publisher assume no responsibility or liability to any entity or person for any errors or omissions, or for any damage or loss caused, or alleged to be caused, directly or indirectly, for the uses made, or not made, of any information in this book.

No warranties are made, express or implied, with regard to the contents of this publication, its merchantability, or fitness for any particular purpose. This book is sold with the understanding that the author and publisher are not engaged in rendering legal, or any other professional services. If such are required, the assistance of a competent professional should be sought.

This book is not meant to take the place of any government or private publications, or courses of instruction, covering the operation of any motor vehicle, trailer, boat, or engine, or any appurtenances thereto, and related laws, regulations, policies, and recommendations. Neither are the comments made in this book meant to take the place of those of any manufacturer, distributor, or dealer of any products referenced here, either directly or indirectly.

Chapter 1

~~~~~~

Buying and Selling Your Power Boat

> **This chapter provides professional know-how and insider secrets in buying and selling a boat.**

You get an in-depth look at just how these transactions are handled. This will make your dealings in this exciting marketplace more satisfying and fun.

We have included our unique **True Costs of Boat Ownership** matrix at the end of the chapter. This will help you better analyze *all* the costs involved, and get to the "bottom line" of your boat-ownership responsibilities.

Some First Thoughts

Buying a power boat is exciting business! When you savor all the things you'll soon be doing, your spirits will soar. That new boat rig will offer really great recreational opportunities for you and your family for years to come.

For some people, purchasing a boat is a spur-of-the-moment thing, while other folks think it over for many months. Either way is fine, as there really is no one "correct" way to buy a boat.

> *What matters is that you get a boat that suits your personal requirements, at a price you can afford to pay.*

Now that's easy to say, but sometimes quite difficult to do. The power boat marketplace can be very confusing, with its dynamic excitement and wide variety of very appealing products. While all this is well and good, many of us get overly caught up in all that enthusiasm. This can result in our usually-sharp business acumen going astray in the euphoria induced by all the gleaming glass, stainless steel, and gel coat. So we sign on several dotted lines and happily drive off with a new rig in tow, not really knowing all the implications of boat ownership, or for that matter, how to put gas in the thing.

All too often, the end result of this **enthusiastic ignorance** is disappointment. Next comes the loss of some big bucks as that now unwanted boat is sold for dimes on the dollar, or else languishes someplace, steadily losing value. All this need not happen...

Reality Check

Our **Reality Check** will help you view the purchase of either a new or used boat as logically as possible. The **Reality Check** is only as good as what you put into it, so please consider your answers carefully.

How much can you afford to spend for the following:

⚓ full purchase price of the rig?

⚓ price of all the Federally required and other equipment needed for safety?

⚓ full cost of any required tow vehicle modifications, or a new tow vehicle to handle the boat?

TOTAL: _____

To determine your annual costs, complete the **True Costs of Boat Ownership** matrix at the end of this chapter. Then add...

⚓ The estimated cost of any training courses, or other annual costs you anticipate.

TOTAL: _____

The preceding will give you an idea of your financial involvement. In many cases, however, money isn't the problem. Instead, unrealized expectations and unanticipated responsibilities are the main causes of dissatisfaction after a boat purchase.

The following questions will help you clarify some of these important facts. Please candidly answer the following:

⚓ What is your real purpose in buying a boat? (Water skiing, fishing, cruising, diving, swimming, exploring, getting out of the house, picnicking, pleasing your kids...or what?)

⚓ Where will the boat be used? (Rivers, small inland lakes, large reservoirs, coastal, off-shore... or where?)

⚓ How many people and how much gear will you be regularly carrying in the boat?

⚓ What operating features do you want in your boat?

(Top speed, range, acceleration, towing ability, shallow water capabilities, stability while underway and while anchored, low-speed handling characteristics?)

⚓ Can you now safely operate such a boat? If the answer is "No," then how, when, and where will you get qualified?

⚓ Are you able now to safely operate a trailer boat rig on the road and launch ramp? If the answer is "No," then how, when, and where will you get your training?

⚓ How much time will you spend with your rig in normal use and upkeep? Most power boats require a large expenditure of time on a regular basis to keep them shipshape.

⚓ Are you able to perform the required preventive and breakdown maintenance service on the rig?

⚓ If not you, who will be providing this maintenance service, where, and at what cost?

⚓ Where will you be storing the boat? If you store the boat off its trailer, you'll have to make arrangements for the trailer's storage.

Keep the answers to these questions in your back pocket for a while. As you start shopping you may find that you want to change some of your answers as you view the many beautiful boats and hear the salesmen extol their virtues.

Make other list(s) with these changes, but keep the original. Then when you think you are finally ready to buy, sit down and calmly look over all of your lists to help make your final decision. Then just do it!

All this may seem overly structured and simplistic, but when you enter the heady world of boat shopping, your wants and needs can get twisted. Our **Reality Check** can help keep your thinking straight.

Good luck!

Other Important Insights

Involve your family early. Your spouse and kids will probably want to get in on all the boating fun from the very start. Don't deny them this pleasure. Conducting a boat search *entirely* on your own can cause family problems. We can almost guarantee, however, that *not* involving your family will cause you more grief than you want.

Talk to everybody you know who is actually involved with power boating...not sailboating...not commercial fishing...not boat racing...not cruising on the Love Boat...but recreational power boating. If you don't know anybody, go out to the nearest marina and talk to some of the folks who have boats there. Don't be shy about this. Most of us are happy to talk boats any old time. You'll get some great ideas on all the things you can do with a boat, and many recommendations about gear. Ask around and find out all you can from active boaters. It helps more than you may now realize, and you'll meet some real nice folks.

Check your newspaper **classified ads,** shopper's tabloids, and small regional newspapers. They will give you an idea of what the type of boat you're thinking about is selling for in its earlier models. Although this information is most useful when buying in the used-boat market, it will give you a basis for comparison when you start looking at new boats, and a general idea of the recreational boat market and some of the costs involved.

Check to see if there are any **boat shows** in your area. If there are, by all means go and spend at least a day. These shows can be a real education to any boater. You should know, however, that boat shows are really tough for most boat junkies. We challenge any boater to walk down all those rows of great-looking, good-smelling, new boats...cold beer flowing...music playing something from "Top Gun"...without feeling big-time impulses to buy one of those beauties with its special boat show price. But remember...

Big-time impulses can cost big-time bucks.

Slow down! Get all the free literature and business cards you can. Look around at the various makes and models of boats displayed in all their glory. Look to your heart's content, drool all you want, but go home without signing anything.

If you think you're experienced, and are really dead sure of what you want and of the deal being offered, still *think again* before you sign anything...preferably sleep on it. Make sure you *really* know what you're doing before you haul out the checkbook.

Here are a couple of other thoughts about boat buying you should keep in mind:

Always ask for a deal! Be alert for **demonstrators** or **boat show specials,** discounts on discontinued models, end-of-season clearances, and introductory prices on new models. You will usually pay more at the start of the boating season, and less at the end.

Know that most dealers want to sell their inventory first. Don't let them talk you into buying an in-stock boat that is only close to your needs. Instead, order one that exactly suits you. The wait will be well worth it, for you will get exactly what you want.

Always negotiate your boating purchases as hard as you can. Better deals are always possible. This applies to the El Swanko Boat Dealership in Miami offering that new, gleaming, 55-foot ocean-going cruiser with twin 450 HP Diesels, to Bubba's Beer & Boats in Lower Swamp City offering you a used, fairly clean, 12-foot johnboat with an Ichiban 3.3 HP engine clinging to the transom. If you don't make every effort to pay the lowest possible price for your rig, you'll be tossing big bucks over the side.

We recommend that you purchase a boat manufactured by a well-established American company. While there certainly isn't anything against boats built overseas, most American power boat buyers are better off with a boat from an established U.S. manufacturer. This is because boats built by American companies usually hold their value better, and are much easier to sell when it's trade-in time.

Check out any boat both on the trailer and in the water. Make certain that your dealer gives you and your family a **test ride** in the type of boat you are considering. That boat must feel right to you and yours during the ride. If you just aren't sure after the ride, say good-bye to that deal and look for something else. It may take a little more time to find just what you want, but it sure beats paying a lot of bucks for a rig in which you don't feel completely comfortable. You would be amazed how many otherwise-savvy business people will buy a boat off the showroom floor without an in-water demonstration. Similarly, we have seen folks buy a boat right after an in-water demo without checking out its trailer, how the boat rides on that trailer, the boat's warranties, reputation, or anything else. While buying any boat rig is pretty heady stuff, with glowing promises of a lot of fun times ahead, you really should make sure that at least a little of your normal business acumen remains intact during this period. Speaking of that...

It may seem a bit too much to be thinking about the future at this point, but you can save yourself some big bucks in the long run if you buy a boat that has a good reputation in your part of the country. Resale time will eventually come for that new boat. If it is a popular make and model it'll move a lot faster, and for a lot higher price, especially if it is favorably known in your market.

Figure 1. _Bayliner 2859 Classic Cruiser._ The cruiser is the largest and fanciest of the trailer boats. Depending on the overall hull size it can sport the most elegant of furnishings and equipment. Fixed bunks, private heads, a complete galley, and air conditioning and heating systems are available. _Photograph courtesy of US Marine._

Figure 2. *Bayliner 1851 Capri Runabout.* The runabout is a very popular recreational power boat design. Its forward deck can be open or covered, and there is a windscreen with side glass/plastic panels. It is enjoyed for its water skiing and other fun-in-the-sun possibilities. *Photograph courtesy of US Marine.*

Figure 3. *Maxum 2000 SR Bowrider Runabout.* The bowrider is the open version of the runabout, with a seating space forward of a walk-through windshield. This design provides additional space for activities such as fishing and water skiing. *Photograph courtesy of US Marine.*

Figure 4. Bayliner 2252 Cuddycabin. The cuddycabin, usually a little larger than the runabout, features a "cuddy," the below deck area forward of the windshield. This space often contains a pair of bunks, a table, storage areas, and other amenities. *Photograph courtesy of US Marine.*

Figure 5. *Robalo 2520 Center Console*. The center console is a very popular boat, used primarily for fishing because of the room. In the "tunnel hull" design it is ideal for shallow water operations. *Photograph courtesy of US Marine.*

Figure 6. Bayliner 2359 Deckboat. The deck boats have become increasingly popular in recent years. Their wide beam and stability make them ideally suited both entertaining afloat, diving, and fishing. *Photograph courtesy of US Marine.*

Figure 7. Bayliner 2502 Walkaround. As the name implies, the walkaround model enables a fisherman, battling that Big One, to move completely around the boat to play the fish. With a "deep-V" hull, walkarounds are widely used on large inland lakes and near off-shore waters. *Photograph courtesy of US Marine.*

Figure 8. Bayliner JAZZ Personal Watercraft. The popular personal watercraft are between 10 and 14 feet in length overall, with a beam of about 6 feet. They are powered by one or two jet engines. These boats are tremendously responsive, can turn within their own length, and are stable enough for fishing or diving. *Photograph courtesy of US Marine.*

Figure 9. *Bayliner 2352 Walkaround.* Note that there are many pleasure boat designs that combine the attributes of boat types. For example, a walkaround could have a cuddycabin as pictured in the boat above. *Photograph courtesy of US Marine*

You now may say, "Whoa, I can't afford a new boat, but I sure want to get on the water, so it's a used boat for me." Fine, we've got a really great section on used boats up ahead, but please read what follows to get a feel for how a new boat purchase is handled. It'll give you some mighty good ideas for buying not only a new boat, but also that used one.

Buying a New Rig

Visit the boat **dealerships** in your immediate area that carry the boats you like. While you are there, look around, ask a lot of questions, see what they have to offer. Take any and all literature available. It would be helpful if a knowledgeable boating friend joined you on these visits. We recommend that you deal with an established dealership which has a fully equipped service department. Work with a sales person with whom you feel comfortable. Be up front about what you want and what you can pay. Here's what you're probably going to be buying:

1. The **Boat**
2. The **Engine** and **Propeller**
3. The **Trailer,** with mounted spare wheel, winch, stand, and necessary boat tie downs
4. **Warranties**—Manufacturer's and Extended
5. **Financing**—Many dealers will arrange financing through a local bank.
6. **Make-Ready Charges**—The dealer will set up the boat, install the engine, rig the boat and trailer.
7. **Equipment—Coast Guard-required** gear so you can legally launch your boat
8. **Insurance**—Most dealers can help you by suggesting a reliable local agent.

In the following pages we show you several of the most popular power boat types. These specialized designs provide a high level of efficiency and enjoyment for the purposes for which they were designed. The next sections will give you some of the general design details about these boats.

Hull Designs

The most popular power boat hull designs are the **deep-V, modified deep-V, tri-hull,** and the **flat bottom**.

The deep-V hull is shaped like a "V" looking aft from the bow. The angle of the "V" from the horizontal at its widest point is the hull's **"deadrise."** The deep-V hull offers a relatively smooth ride as it cuts through the waves. The deep-V design also causes the boat to be lifted as it moves forward through the water. A boat is then said to be "planing" or "on plane" when at its design "planing speed." The deep-V is widely used in off-shore boats. It rides best while on plane. At rest, or at very low speeds, it rocks to an extent determined by its beam and length, and the water and wind conditions.

The modified deep-V hull is perhaps the most common small power boat design. It features the deep-V configuration at the front of the hull, flattening out rapidly toward the stern. At cruise speeds, the bow end cuts through the waves, producing a stable ride. The flat-bottom area aft provides improved stability at low speeds and at rest. Increased boat speeds are possible with this design, as the hull lifts substantially out of the water when on plane, which reduces total drag.

The tri-hull, or cathedral hull, is essentially three V-hulls joined side-by-side. It is exceptionally stable and pleasant in smooth water. When it's rough, however, this hull produces a rough ride and much spray. Nevertheless, the tri-hull is popular among some inland lake and river fishermen, and among many boaters wanting a stable platform while at rest in calmer waters.

The flat-bottom boat is used in a variety of pleasure and commercial applications. It is very popular for use on quieter waters, although it can be seen all over the place in a wide variety of conditions. It does not cut through the water while underway, but instead rides high on top. It produces a stable ride under calm conditions, but when the water gets rough you'll feel like you're riding a wild bull...which is not a bad sport.

In its wider configurations the **johnboat** is an excellent fishing platform, if the water is relatively calm. As this great hull is not really designed for speed, smaller outboard engines are usually utilized.

Hull Construction

The design of a boat's hull, and the material used in its construction, is determined by the hull strength required, and the size and type of boat.

Most modern power boats are manufactured of **fiberglass.** This economical, inert, flexible material provides excellent durability and low maintenance costs. Fiberglass boat construction techniques have been in practice for many years. The boat's rigid, outer hull is created in a mold using resin reinforced fiberglass materials.

The three principle types of hull and deck construction are **chopper gun, hand layup,** and **solid fiberglass.** A core between the layers of fiberglass provides increased strength to the hull. The main types of cores presently being used by boat manufacturers are **balsa, foam,** and **plywood.**

The modern hull is built up in layers in a mold...the base **roving** (a thick woven fabric for puncture strength)...

then the **mat** (random chopped fibers in a layer for bulk)... then **fiberglass cloth** (provides a reinforcing surface)...and finally, the **gel coat** (the slick, outer finish).

Other structural members of the boat are fabricated in a like manner. These are the bulkheads, consoles, transoms, decks, casting platforms, and the like.

Aluminum hulls have been extremely popular over the years as an economical and efficient material for power boat construction. Construction techniques usually involve the riveting or welding of the various hull components into the desired shapes. Welded aluminum boats are extremely durable and widely used, particularly in adverse operating conditions.

Power boats are, of course, made of other materials, such as plywood or wooden planking. These are not discussed here as they are not in general use.

Inspecting a New Boat

Here are a few basic things to consider as you look at various new boats:

Can your car or truck readily tow the boat rig in the areas you'll be traveling?

Are you certain you can operate the boat in the waters you have in mind? It takes a certain skill level to operate any boat safely. The bigger the boat and bigger the water, the more skill is required.

Can the boat function well where you'll be primarily operating? For example, a big deep-V can't operate well in the flats, or up some shallow river. Nor can a flats or river boat safely go off-shore.

Is the boat's general appearance pleasing to you? Is the external hull finish what you want?

Is the boat's internal finish what you like? If it is carpeted, is the carpet a top-quality, sun-resistant, marine-grade fabric? Is it securely glued to the deck and the other carpeted parts? Will it be easy to keep clean? Is the upholstery of good quality, and sun-resistant to preclude early fading?

How about the metal fittings and fasteners on the boat? They should be high-grade stainless steel, or bronze, to avoid corrosion problems. This is particularly important if you will be using your boat in or around brackish or salt water. Most ferrous-based metals, other than stainless steel, soon dissolve in salt water. (An easy way to tell if something is *not* stainless steel is to put a magnet on the article. If the magnet sticks, the article is not stainless.)

Are there an adequate number of **cleats?** You'll need one at the boat's centerline on the bow, and one on each gunwale fore and aft, plus one or more amidships on each side. These should be stainless steel, bronze, or the highest quality marine grade plastic. They should be thru-bolted with stainless steel bolts and lock nuts.

Check at least one of the cleats for proper installation during your inspection of the boat. The length of the cleat should be about 16 times the diameter of the line to be used. For example, if you use ½-inch diameter line you'll need 8-inch long cleats. Some new boats sport dinky little pot-metal cleats that you may want to have replaced before you take delivery.

Carefully check any **thru-hull** and **thru-bulkhead fittings.** Make sure they are of stainless steel or heavy plastic construction, and have been solidly installed. The holes they are in must be silicon sealed.

Is the **bow eye** made of stainless steel and thru-bolted with reinforced backing inside the boat?

Check the boat's interior layout. Are there enough seats for the number of people who will regularly be aboard the vessel?

Will your projected load exceed the carrying capacity of the hull? Check the metal plate fastened on the hull to determine the Coast Guard-approved **load limits** in number of persons and total weight. If you regularly want to take more folks aboard than the hull can legally carry, you need a larger boat.

If there is an enclosed **head,** do the sit-down/lean-forward/stand-up test with the door closed to make sure you can fit.

If there is a **live well,** how is it drained and filled? Is it large enough for your bait/catch? Can you get at it easily?

Is there enough storage for the life jackets (PFDs), one per passenger? Are life jackets instantly accessible?

Is there enough **storage space** for all the gear you'll be carrying? Are the storage areas easily accessible?

The storage situation on every boat can be quickly summed up...there's never enough. Your gear will soon fill every nook and cranny. So look at all the available storage and visualize how you will use it. Will you be able to get at your gear with reasonable ease while underway? Are there conflicts between where people sit and where you want to store things? Where will you stow the big, clumsy gear like your rods, water skis, tubes, and other water toys?

Check the boat's electrical system carefully. Problems there can be a persistent headache.

Is the boat's **electrical system** adequate for the uses you plan? Is the boat's 12-volt wiring properly color-coded? Ask your dealer to explain this to you and show you on the boat.

Is any of the boat's wiring running through places where water accumulates? If so, how is it safeguarded against shorts?

Personally locate *all* the **fuses/circuit breakers.** Check to make sure that you could get at them in rough weather and at night. We recommend that your boat be equipped with circuit breakers in place of fuses to the maximum extent possible. The small, additional cost up front will be repaid many times over, in time saved and aggravation avoided, during the life of the boat.

Are the best quality, maintenance-free **marine batteries** installed for engine cranking and electronic device purposes? Can *you* get at them handily? Are they in approved battery boxes, and rigidly secured with heavy duty hold-downs? They should not be able to move more than 1 inch in any direction.

Are the batteries' **CCA (Cold Cranking Amperes)** adequate? See your engine manual for the requirements. Is the battery **RTM (Reserve Time in Minutes)** adequate for the total electrical load to be placed on the system? If you have questions, ask the sales rep to compute this for your system.

IMPORTANT

If there is a 115/120-volt panel aboard for a shoreside connection, it must be located separately from the boat's 12-volt panel.

Now sit at the boat's **helm.** Are you comfortable? Can you easily see all around when you are afloat? There are many boats that afford little visibility from a seated position at the helm. This is not satisfactory. Good visibility to all sides is imperative.

Can you reach all the controls easily while at the helm? Check all the switches and what they control. While at the helm, check all the electric and electronic fixtures on the boat to make sure they really work.

Figure 10. *Outboard Engine.* The outboard engine has been popular since the early part of this century. Developed originally by Mr. Ole Evinrude to push his fishing boat around, the outboard engine has grown steadily in sophistication and power.

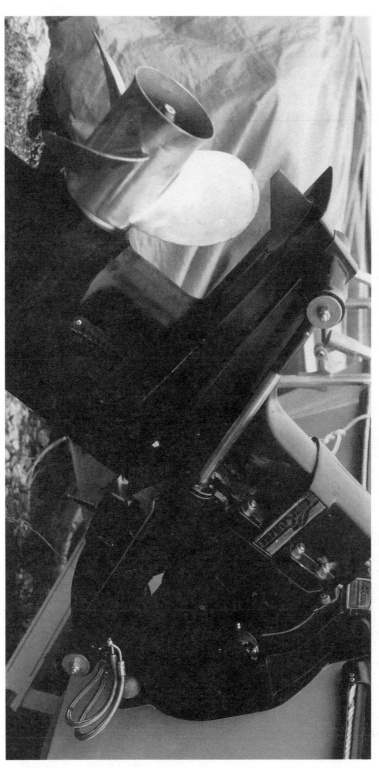

Figure 11. _Inboard/Outboard Engine._ The popular Inboard/Outboard (I/O) engine has been around for many years. The "inboard" component is usually a marine-adapted automotive-type power plant. It is solidly bolted down, many times under an upholstered box in the aft section of the boat. The "outboard" unit shown here is mounted on the boat's transom. It is raised and lowered hydraulically from the helm.

Figure 12. *Jet Engine.* The jet engine has been in use for many years and is a proven power plant. The power source is a standard marine engine driving a turbine which sucks in water and expels it out the stern, shown above. Note the "clam shell" which is lowered from the helm to cause reverse thrust. The unit is moved from side-to-side for directional control.

Does the boat have adequate **instrumentation?** For the four-cycle engine (inboard and I/O), you'll need at least a tachometer, engine temperature gauge, oil pressure gauge, and an ammeter.

On a two-cycle engine (most outboards), a tachometer and engine-head temperature gauge are the bare minimum.

For **navigation,** you'll need a good quality magnetic compass mounted on, or very near, the boat's centerline, where it can easily be seen at the helm.

What kind of **fuel tank** does the boat have?

IMPORTANT

Is that fuel tank large enough for the type of boat and engine, and your projected uses of the boat? Too small a tank could severely limit your range of operations, besides being a pain to refill every couple of hours.

Is the tank easily accessible? If not, how will you replace itwhen it starts to leak? Will you have to tear out any part of the boat to get at the thing, or can it be replaced with no major effort?

Can you get at the fuel tank filler neck easily to put fuel in your boat? Is there an installed overflow vent? If not, where do the fuel spills go when you overfill the tank, or when the temperature rises and the fuel tank overflows?

How about the **engine oil?** What system is used to deliver oil to the engine? Is it a reliable, proven method? Will you be able to buy oil in bulk from your boat dealer, and realize a significant savings?

Are there adequately sized **water tanks** aboard the boat? This is important on boats with installed plumbing systems.

Are all components that need regular service easily accessible? Can you get at them without having to disassemble a lot of stuff to work on them?

What has to be done to the boat and engine when the temperature goes below freezing? Can you personally do it or does it require your dealer's expert skills?

Are good quality **bilge pumps** installed? Do they drain the entire bilge? Are the pumps manually switched on, or are they automatic? If automatic, is the switch proven to be reliable? In case of switch failure, can the pumps safely run "dry" after all the bilge water has been pumped out?

Are the **drain plugs** easy to put in and take out? We suggest *you* actually take them out and put them back in. Do they drain the entire bilge or only the aft sections?

The Engine

There are essentially four types of engines used in power boating. These are the **Outboard Engine,** the **Inboard Engine,** the **Inboard/Outboard (I/O) Engine,** and the **Jet Engine.** Each of these are effective in a wide variety of applications.

We have no real bias on engine types, except for leaning slightly toward the outboard. It affords maximum room in the cockpit, with ease of access for servicing, plus lots of power. Outboards are also great for shallow water use as they can be mounted high on the transom and trimmed way up.

Both the I/O and inboards work fine for most applications, except for extreme shallow water operations. Inboard boats require a special trailer design because of their fixed propellers and rudders.

The jet engine is widely used with good results in many parts of the United States. This power plant uses the same power source as the propeller-drive engine, with the jet drive unit replacing the propeller. Note that there is about a 30 percent loss in effective power compared to the propeller-equipped engine. Thus a standard 150 HP engine driving a jet unit will produce about the same force on the water as a standard 110 HP engine. There is no real problem here, as long as you don't expect the same results from a jet unit as you would get from a propeller at the same horsepower rating.

Another concern is that the jet engine powered boat has reduced directional control at low speeds. This lack of positive, low speed directional control can be a problem in close quarters and around other boat traffic, and when you are trying to get your jet boat back onto its trailer.

However, there are many applications where a jet is the best power source to be had. Its use in shallow Western and Midwestern rivers is widespread and very popular. Our experience has been that the jets work best on flat-bottom boats.

Jets are also being widely used on personal watercraft, as shown earlier, and on jet skis. You can use your jet to hose down your friends once you learn how to jack your boat around, but don't tell anybody you got that here.

Ask your dealer to explain the merits of the various engines and to suggest the right type for the boating you will be doing most of the time. Be guided by the dealer's recommendations, absent any compelling reason to the contrary.

In your selection process, please be certain that the engine installed on the boat you are considering is of adequate power for your purposes. An under-powered boat can be very disappointing. If there is any doubt, negotiate for the installation of an engine at, or near, the maximum rated horsepower for the hull you are buying. This horsepower rating information appears on the metal "Capacity" plate permanently fastened to the boat. The larger engine will initially cost more than the amount quoted for some "package deals" with a smaller engine, but it sure is worth the price in terms of satisfaction, and in resale value when that time comes.

WARNING

Although we recommend adequately powering your boat, there is a very real danger in over-powering. Installing too large an engine for a hull is dangerous. Never install an engine exceeding the Coast Guard limitation for that hull.

Propellers

A marine propeller is a essentially a **water screw.** When turned by the engine, it expels water off its blade surfaces. When the propeller is "looking" aft, this motion of the expelled water to the rear causes a forward-thrusting force which is transmitted to the boat, causing it to move forward. It's good to keep in mind that the propeller is the only means by which the horsepower your expensive engine generates is put to useful work. This power is transmitted from the engine's **powerhead,** by shafts and gearing, to the propeller.

Now let's look at a few facts about the propeller. As you may know, they are made of several materials—usually **aluminum, stainless steel,** or **high-impact plastic.**

Aluminum propellers are popular for the average boat under average conditions. They are available in almost every size and configuration at reasonable cost. We have found them easy to damage, but cheap to repair. However, after years of making the propeller rebuild folks grin as they planned their winter trip to the Bahamas over our

Figure 13. *Single Axle Boat Trailer.* This is a typical single-axle drive-on boat trailer. Note the spare wheel location.

battered props, we recently converted to stainless steel, and are much more satisfied.

Stainless steel propellers possess excellent strength-to-weight ratios. They are widely popular and available in a wide range of types. They are more expensive than the aluminum, but are much more durable. As they are manufactured with thinner blades, due to their greater strength, they are much more efficient than aluminum.

High-impact plastic propellers are available in a wide variety of sizes and types. They are useful for light loads, and as "get-home" replacements.

Many engines come equipped by the dealer with a stock, three-bladed propeller. This is adequate for a wide variety of general boating purposes. On large engines under heavy loads, a four-bladed prop will give good results. If you are into boat racing, there's a five-blade propeller available. It all depends on the uses you plan for your boat, and how deep your pockets are.

Closely related to the number of blades on your propeller is its **diameter** and **pitch.** The diameter is the straight line distance from the extreme outer edge of the blades through the propeller's center. The pitch is the distance advanced in the water by the propeller in one revolution, assuming no slippage. Together with the propeller's diameter, the pitch influences the RPM that a particular engine can develop. Generally speaking, a heavy boat designed for relatively slow operation will use a lesser pitch propeller than a lighter, faster boat.

The propeller that is right for your boat is the one that lets your engine put out its maximum-rated RPM. You don't want a propeller, however, that allows the engine to run above its maximum-rated RPM, as engine damage could result. You should know that a propeller that will not permit the engine to develop its maximum RPM can be more damaging than one that allows excessive RPM.

This is because excessive engine torque develops, putting stresses above design limits on the engine's power train. You can easily control overrevs with the throttle, but not overtorque.

Talk to your boat dealer to get ideas on which type and size of propeller is right for your particular application. Then get the best quality propeller you can afford. Remember, the propeller is the only means your engine has to deliver all that high-priced horsepower.

The Jack Plate

This is a hydraulic device to raise and lower the entire outboard engine. The engine is bolted to its movable bracket, which is then mounted on a fixed base fastened to the boat's transom. The entire movable bracket can be moved up and down from the helm. The total amount of this vertical travel is about 6 inches. They are moved in conjunction with trimming the boat in many cases.

Jack plates are usually hydraulically-powered, but there are manual models around for use on small outboards.

The jack plate originally evolved as a solution to difficulties experienced in mounting outboard engines of varying shaft lengths on boats of different transom heights. Some rather interesting performance improvements became evident, however, and their use spread. It was found, for example, that on some boats speed increases of 1.0 to 1.5 mph are possible for every inch that the engine is raised.

Many Skippers use their jack plate to lower the engine so that its cavitation plate, a horizontal flat plate on the engine shaft located just above the propeller, is about level with the bottom of the boat, or even lower, to get the best control for low speed maneuvering.

The engine is raised during the **hole shot** (that period of time from moving the throttle to full open to when the boat comes up on plane). After the boat is up and planing, the jack plate is usually at its highest position.

Please note that the effective use of a jack plate may take some practice and experience.

The Trailer

It is extremely important to buy the right trailer for your boat. The overall length and gross weight of your boat, including the boat's engine, filled fuel and water tanks, and all the gear you normally carry in your boat when on the road, directly influence the trailer type and size.

Usually as the boat's length increases, its gross weight increases. As this weight increases, the load-carrying capacity of the two-tire trailer is reached at around 2,500 pounds. It will then be necessary to either consider a smaller boat, or else get a two-axle trailer.

If you are within 100 pounds of the trailer's rated capacity with your load, get the next larger trailer size. The **Capacity Plate** on the trailer's tongue will show its rated capacity, tire size and pressure, and other manufacturer's information.

Most trailers use **rollers** or **padded bunks,** either singly, or in some combination, to support the boat. We feel that rollers are best for a trailer if the boat is 16 feet or longer. Ask your dealer about the specifics for your area and boating practices.

Your trailer should have adequate side supports to keep the boat laterally centered. These should be adjusted by the dealer to properly fit the hull of your boat. The trailer must have a bow post that supports the winch and holds the bow of the boat firmly in place.

IMPORTANT

To avoid serious structural damage, your boat must never overhang the rear support member of the trailer.

Here are some important trailer questions:

Is the trailer's rated capacity adequate for the load you will be carrying? That load will be the gross weight of your boat and engine, plus the gear you will be carrying in the boat. Don't forget to include the weight of the engine fuel and drinking water carried in your boat's tanks. Gasoline weighs about 6.2 pounds per gallon, and water about 8.3 pounds per gallon.

Is the trailer fully galvanized throughout? If not, rust and corrosion will seriously shorten its life. A properly primed, painted trailer is usable in fresh water, but around salt it will corrode very rapidly.

Is the trailer's **tongue** long enough to allow you to put your truck's tailgate down all the way?

Can you fully **jackknife** the loaded trailer on your tow vehicle without jerking the safety chains, pulling out the trailer wiring connection, or hitting the boat with the tow vehicle?

Is the trailer **wiring** easy to get to for service? Is it secured to the trailer frame? Is the trailer separately fused from the tow vehicle? Is the trailer's connector to the tow vehicle's electrical system solid and easy to use? Are all the required lights on the trailer?

Are the lights rated as submersible? We've never seen a fixture that really holds out the water after just a little bit of service. Every one of them seems to fail after a relatively short time. Salt water makes it a lot worse. You can help matters some, and delay the inevitable a little, by hosing down your trailer with fresh water immediately after using it in salt water.

When a light bulb goes out on the trailer, do you have to replace a whole light unit, or can you easily stick in just a spare bulb? Are those bulbs readily available?

Importantly, is there a spare wheel? Are the lug nuts or bolts standard size, or do you need to buy a special wrench? Is the spare tire new and properly inflated? Will your tow vehicle jack lift and support the loaded trailer so you can change a flat tire on the trailer? Many car or truck jacks won't fit a boat trailer, and a separate jack is required. Find out about this before you go on the road.

When the loaded trailer is connected to your tow vehicle, will its tongue be about parallel to the ground? If not, the dealer should recommend an appropriate solution. Stability problems can arise on the highway if there is a serious misfit.

Will the trailer's **safety chains** fit on your vehicle? A good fit is when they are long enough that you can make a full jack-knife with the rig and not jerk on the chains, but yet not so long that they drag on the ground when you're driving straight ahead.

How about the wiring connection into the vehicle's electrical system? Is the lead long enough that you can fully jackknife without pulling out the connector, but not so long that it drags? Is that connector solid and easy to use in the dark, and with gloves?

Is the **coupler** the same size as the ball on your tow vehicle? If it isn't, you're going to have to change out that ball before you use the trailer.

Does the trailer have a high quality **jack** mounted on the tongue? Does it crank easily? Is it long enough that you can crank the boat to a slight (about 2 inches) bow high position, so water in the bilge goes out the stern drain(s)? Does the wheel spin around off the ground while you're cranking, requiring you to hold it with your foot? This is not a fatal problem, but it sure is annoying to stand there cranking away, holding that dumb wheel with your big toe.

How about the **winch?** Is it good quality, solid metal, or some plastic junker? It's pretty hard to tell about this, so we feel the best way is to insist on an all-metal, heavily galvanized, American-built winch. It should crank easily and have an adequate gear ratio capacity to easily pull your boat. If you are getting a heavier boat, say one over 20 feet, you may want to install an **electric winch** with a remote control. Some folks suggest an electric winch for *any* size boat. Ask your dealer.

Is there a new **winch line, steel cable,** or **nylon strap** on the winch? If you're going into salt water, you will soon rust out a steel cable. A nylon rope will weaken, fray, and then break after a few months' use. We recommend a nylon strap for use in both fresh and salt water. Plan on replacing it about every year due to UV deterioration from the sun.

Check the **tie-down straps.** You must secure the boat's back end firmly on the trailer. One way is a strap across the boat's **beam** (the direction across the boat at right angles to its long axis) about one-quarter the way up from the **transom.** Another way is to use two tie-down straps, running from the **water-ski towing eyes** on the boat's transom to eye bolts on the right and left main beams of the trailer frame. You also should have a strap, light chain, or line from the **bow eye** (fastening point on the bow) to the forward part of the trailer's frame. This is an important safety item in that this restraint keeps the boat from climbing into the tow vehicle in the event of a front-end collision.

Warranties

You should clearly understand the terms of the **factory warranties** and **guarantees** for the new items you are buying. Discuss these with your dealer if you have any questions before you leave the premises.

After you get home, we recommend that you gather all the warranty and guarantee paperwork and keep it in one safe place. For some perverse reason, these papers always seem to get mislaid.

Your new boat's **hull** will usually carry a warranty good for several years. The terms differ among the various manufacturers, but generally provide repair or replacement for certain types of faults at the manufacturer's expense for a stipulated time period. Five years is common.

The new engine warranties also vary with the manufacturer, but usually provide coverage for parts and labor for a specified period. One year is common.

New trailer warranties are usually for a one-year period for labor and parts. The **tires** are usually covered under a separate warranty with varying types of tread-wear and other coverages depending on their manufacturer. Please buy American-made tires specifically designed for boat trailer use.

You should go over the warranties carefully with your dealer before you close on any deal. This is important because you can almost bet that something will go wrong in the first months you have your new rig, and you don't want to get unnecessarily nailed for a big repair bill. You must know your rights!

Extended warranties give you coverage against certain hazards arising *after* the original purchase warranty runs out. They are sold by both the manufacturer of the item through dealerships, and by third parties.

When you buy an extended warranty you are "betting" you will need the repairs the warranty covers. The issuer of the warranty is "betting" that repairs won't be needed. The amount of your bet is the premium you pay. The amount of the issuer's bet is what they pay out if the item breaks.

Based on our experience, it makes economic sense to buy this extended coverage on your boat's engine for a year or two after its original warranty runs out.

Financing

Most of us just can't pay cash up front for a new boating rig. These can start around $10,000 and go way, way up. This means that we have to borrow the funds if we want to get on the water.

A **loan** on a boating rig is available from the same places you get an automobile loan...your family, banks, credit unions, savings and loans, and certain retail credit companies. It will definitely pay to shop around for your loan. The total cost of the loan will consist of the principal amount you borrow, the interest charges applied to that, plus the closing and other loan initiation costs. Your boat dealer may also offer financing. This you certainly should consider, comparing all the costs involved with the other loan sources.

Be aware that the **depreciation** rate on new boats is extremely high. This means that when you drive out of your dealer's premises with that new boat in tow, the boat's value takes a real nose dive. If you have taken out a long-term loan for most of the purchase price of the rig, there could be a problem if you attempt to re-sell that boat during the early life of the loan.

A typical case would be if you wanted to buy a new boat after a year or so of paying on your first rig. When you try to negotiate a trade for your first boat, its market value could be substantially less than what you paid for it. The result would be that you would have to put up out-of-pocket cash to pay off the first loan. This is because the current market value of the first boat wouldn't be enough to cover the amount still owed on the loan contract.

This situation tends to occur when there is a glut of used boats on the market, with low demand driving their prices down. This is usually coupled with a shortage of more desirable new boats, with high demand driving prices up.

Make-Ready

It costs the dealer quite a few bucks to take a new boat straight from the factory, off the delivering carrier, and get it ready for your use. Depending on what you've ordered installed on the rig, many man-hours are expended. The entire unit must be carefully unpacked, cleaned, inspected, and rigged. The engine and its controls must be installed and test run. **Electronics** need to be installed and tested. The trailer needs to be set up, and made road-worthy.

These dealer service costs are passed on to you as "make-ready" charges, or some similar name. They are a completely legitimate cost, and are mentioned here to explain what can seem to be yet another cryptic entry on your already mind-boggling invoice.

Delivery Day

With all the wheeling and dealing completed, you are now finally going to get that brand new rig in your hands. Let's see how the Big Day usually plays out, so you won't have too many surprises.

We'll assume now that everything is OK, and the dealer called and said it's time to come pick up your new Pride and Joy. You, and your experienced boating friend (ideally), arrive at the boat dealer's at the appointed hour. After contacting your sales rep, you are walked out to where your new boat is parked. There she is, all shiny and new, gleaming in the sunshine or rain, as the case may be. Now it's time for you to go over that new boat, engine, and trailer with a fine-toothed comb. Don't listen when the sales rep says, "So-long, friend, it's been a pleasure. Your boat is all OK. Just add water." Make the rep stay, and/or get somebody from management, to audit the invoice with you line by line.

IMPORTANT

Make sure the items you are buying, as shown on the invoice, are really there. Take nobody's word. Check the rig against the invoice item by item. Big bucks are about to change hands. You want to be sure you're really getting everything you're paying for. When you're satisfied that everything is correctly billed, ask to be shown how everything works. Don't be bashful about this, or try to pretend that you're some sort of boating expert. Find out as much as you can before you leave the dealer's.

Then check everything: all the controls, all the boat's lights, and installed electronics. Tilt the engine, or outdrive, through its full range, and then secure it for highway travel. If there is a jack plate installed, run it through its full range. Locate *all* the fuses and/or circuit breakers.

Find out about engine fuel. Is there a problem using a gasoline augmented by **alcohol** in your engine? Check the amount of fuel in the tank(s) now to see if you'll have to fuel up before you launch. Do you really know how to put the fuel in the tank? If not, have them show you.

How about the **engine oil?** Do you know what type you need, and how to get it into the engine? If it is to be pre-mixed, as on the smaller outboard engines, have the dealer show you how to do this. If the oil is to be put into a separate reservoir, have the dealer show you about that, how it works, and the kind of oil you must use.

After you've checked the boat and engine, take a good look at the trailer. Back your tow vehicle into position and see exactly how the hook-up is made to the trailer. Then hook it up yourself, with help as required by the dealer. Personally connect the safety chains and the electrical connector.

After the hook-up, make sure that everything is connected properly. Is the coupler all the way down on the ball, with its latch down and locked? Are the **safety chains** in position and correctly attached to the tow vehicle? Do all the trailer lights really work?

Take a tire gauge and check the **trailer tires.** On a single-axle trailer, the pressure should be around 35 pounds. For a trailer with more than one axle, ask your dealer. Check the **spare tire** for proper inflation and mounting on its carrier.

Is the boat ready for the upcoming road trip? Are the tie downs all in place? Is the bow secured? Is the winch strap tight? Is everything secured inside the boat? Is the engine in the travel position and properly braced per the Engine Owner's Manual?

Are the boat's **drain plugs** in the boat? Are they the right size? *You* should actually put them in and take them out if you haven't done this before.

Now, if all these things work out OK, you should be ready to say so-long to your dealer and head on out. Before you depart, though, say hello to the **Service Manager.** This is a person with whom you will soon be developing a relationship as things begin to go wrong with your rig. Also, you must know when your new rig should be returned to the dealer for the **scheduled inspections.**

As the new engine must be broken in properly, ask the Service Manager just what you have to do, or not do, during the first hours of operation. All this, of course, is in your Engine Owner's Manual, but ask the Service Manager anyway. Let him get to know you. Impress on him that you want personal assistance to keep your new rig in top condition.

After you take delivery of your new boat, contact your local **Coast Guard Auxiliary (USCGA)** and request a **Courtesy Marine Examination (CME).** This free exam is conducted by specially trained volunteers. It is designed to point out any safety defects in your boat and its equipment. In the process you'll meet some very wise and knowledgeable people who can be of great assistance in your boating. Call the **U.S. Coast Guard Hotline** at **1-800-368-5647** for your Auxiliary's telephone number.

Boat Sales Methods

Most boat dealerships offer essentially two ways of buying a new rig. In the first, the dealer assembles the rig from a stock of boats, trailers, and engines. If some item you want is not in stock, the dealer orders it for you. The dealer then assembles the rig for you. This method is used when a buyer has unique requirements.

The second method involves factory-assembled and delivered units consisting of the boat, engine, and trailer, all marketed together at one "package" price. These package deals are offered by most large boat manufacturers through their dealerships at prices that may be lower than for a comparable rig assembled from the dealer's stock. This marketing method is very popular with many new boaters, as the components of the package are matched by factory experts, thus reducing the number of decisions the boat buyer has to make.

Some excellent buys can be made with such package arrangements; however, there are several things to be sure about before you sign on any dotted lines:

First, be certain that the boat you're considering is the one you really want, and not almost what you want. The few bucks and hours that you save buying a package deal may not be worth it, if what you get isn't right for you.

Secondly, you also should be positive that the **engine** offered is right for what you want the boat to do for you. The engine should be at, or very close to, the maximum rated engine for that hull.

Thirdly, the **trailer** being offered should preferably come from your boat's manufacturer. Some local dealers buy their trailers separately because of lower prices, and/or reduced freight costs. Such a trailer may not be exactly right for the boat involved.

Buying a Used Rig

If you decide to buy a previously-owned boat from another individual, or from a boat dealer, you will join that very large group of folks who regularly and very happily do just that. Please be guided by what we've just told you about buying a new boat, as most of those comments can apply to the purchase of a used boat.

You also should become familiar with the **bureaucratic requirements** where you live regarding the transfer of ownership of boats, engines, trailers, and related items. There are usually transfer and registration fees of some sort to be paid. When you buy a new boat the dealer usually takes care of all this, but when you deal with an individual seller, you're on your own with your State Boating Office.

Having said all that, let's now assume that you've located a rig that appears to be what you want.

Be aware that what you see is usually what you get, and that what you don't see can be a problem. There is usually no warranty or guarantee. The first thing you should research is the price of the rig. A good reference is the annual **"USED BOAT DIRECTORY,"** published by BUC International Corporation, Ft. Lauderdale, Florida. Most dealers will have this publication readily at hand, but you may not easily get the information you want. Some just don't want to talk price about something they're not selling.

Check out the used boats advertised in the **classified** pages of your local newspapers. Note any that match the rig you've decided on, and get a price quote from the advertisers.

The purpose of all this is to get a price range. Keep in mind, though, that each boat will probably have aboard certain equipment that must be kept separate from the price of the boat. Although lumping everything together in a boat sale is quite common, you usually are better off keeping things segregated, and getting separate prices.

This equipment consists of life jackets, tools, water toys, water-ski towing harnesses, anchors, lines, spot lights, mirrors, radios, installed electronics, compasses, etc. Plus anything added to the hull, such as transducers, trim tabs, swim steps, bimini tops, boat covers, antenna, and so on. The list can be long!

Don't forget the boat's engine and the trailer. Sometimes folks install extra items on these that must be identified as part of any sale.

IMPORTANT

Being sure about all items involved in the deal going in will save you much trouble coming out.

Ask the seller for a look at the **maintenance service records** of the boat, engine, and trailer. If the rig has been maintained in professional service facilities, these records should be readily available. They give you an idea of what went wrong with the rig in the past, and the preventive maintenance performed on it. Most importantly, they give you a good idea whether the seller took proper care of the rig. If the rig has *not* received professional service, we recommend you either reject it, or else proceed with care.

The attitude of the seller can also tell you a lot about the condition of the rig. You should try to find out *why* he is selling the rig, and play on that in your negotiations.

Your first impressions of the rig are significant. There are exceptions, of course, but a junky-looking rig is usually just that. Please note, however, that sometimes a really good boat is hidden under a mess of surface crud. As in many other situations, things may not be what they seem. Don't let a really good deal slip by because the upholstery looks rough, or the carpet is dirty, or the boat smells vaguely of dead fish.

Carefully check the **titles** and **registrations** of the boat, engine, trailer, and other gear, as applicable. It really pays to make sure that you don't get stuck with any expired permit or license renewals. Renewals can get quite costly.

As you examine the titles, registrations and maintenance records, determine if there are any **liens** on any of the items being offered for sale by this seller. This essential information becomes a part of any deal that would result from your negotiations.

Any boat you consider should be checked both in and out of the water. Don't make the mistake of only checking the boat on the trailer. You would be surprised how many otherwise sharp people there are who won't take the time to properly inspect a used rig that strikes their fancy. Then later some really serious and very expensive defect is discovered, and they're stuck with it. There are junker boats out there just like there are junker used cars!

The Used Boat

Stand off a little way and really look at any boat you're thinking about buying. Does she strike your fancy? Why? Why Not? Is it her appearance? Does that humongous engine give you dreams of really tearing up the lake and impressing everybody on the beach? Is it the sleek lines of her hull? Just why does that boat appeal, or not appeal, to you? Think about it!

Now ask yourself if that boat will provide you with the means to do what you want to do on the water. If you aren't sure about any of this, take our **Reality Check** again. If you look at enough boats, and think this way, you will eventually discover what you *really* want in a boat. That's mighty important to discover before you sink a lot of bucks into a rig you just "think" you like.

When you come down to actually inspecting a boat (called **"surveying"**), here are some things to look for:

Stand at the bow, and then the stern, and look down the hull for any irregularities. The surface should be smooth and slick with few, if any, waves in the outer surface. Carefully examine the hull for gouges, cracks, **delamination,** and any penetrations. Note carefully any patches or repairs. If the hull was ever penetrated below the waterline, find out if the repairs were done by a professional marine technician. If not, that hull could be faulty and the source of many future problems.

In examining a **fiberglass** hull, carefully examine the outside of the hull at an angle to check for smoothness of the gel coat and any surface irregularities such as bulges.

Look for any **"basket-weave"** spots on the hull. These may indicate a basic construction problem. Tap a coin lightly around sharp corners on the inside of the hull. You should hear a clean, solid response. If you hear a dull, hollow response, there may be a laminate gel coat separation. Check for any delamination and cracking of the fiberglass. Pay particular attention to areas where the fiberglass encapsulates wooden structures, such as the transom, the bow, and the major structural members of the vessel. If the outer fiberglass surface is penetrated, water can get inside the structure. If wood is there, rot is inevitable, necessitating expensive repairs.

If the boat is made of aluminum, its biggest enemies are cracking, corrosion, and pitting. You should carefully look for these conditions throughout the entire hull, particularly around joints and rivets. Also check for any loose or missing fasteners.

Make sure that the hull and bottom sections are constructed of adequate-strength aluminum. They should feel rigid and solid. Some manufacturers will use light gauge aluminum, which can result in excessive flexing. This can cause early failure of the member due to metal fatigue. Make certain that any aluminum hull you consider has enough heft for your purposes.

Look for quality in any boat you examine. As a general rule, if the visible parts of a boat are soundly constructed of first-grade materials, the parts you can't see are probably the same. If the exterior fittings are not really solid, be cautious about that boat.

Check for any exposed, untreated wood in any **transom cutouts.** Such wood will swiftly deteriorate.

Check for any weak or soft spots in the **deck.** Walk slowly over the entire deck surface, in your stocking feet if possible, feeling as you go for soft spots. These may mean that the deck is rotting and expensive repairs may be required.

In an outboard or I/O, raise the engine, or outer unit, and vigorously attempt to move it from side to side and up and down. Give it a strong shaking. As you are doing this, watch the back of the boat. If the **transom** moves, almost independently of the rest of the hull, this is a sign of bad wood at the transom joints.

Another check is to take a small, slim knife blade and poke the inside of the transom next to any thru-hull fitting. If the knife goes in easily, the wood may be bad.

Check all **wooden seat supports** and **bulkheads** for bad wood. Look at the **upholstery** for fading, tears, and cuts. Check out the **carpet,** if any, for wear, cuts, and cleanliness. Check every compartment and cubby hole for deterioration or rot.

Check the windows for cracks, permanently fogged or **crazed plastic** or glass, and for sturdy locks and latches. All windows should be either made of shatter-proof safety glass or plastic. Make sure all hatch covers and all doors fit snugly and solidly. All instruments should work, and installed electrical gear should function properly.

The Used Engine

Examine the engine carefully. How does it look in general? Is it clean? Has it ever been completely submerged? If it has been submerged, how was it subsequently cared for? If it was overheated, how was it cared for?

Is the finish in good shape, considering the age of the engine? Has the engine been kept outside most of the time? If it has been exposed to below freezing temperatures, was it properly **winterized?** Are there any signs of oil leaks, or any cracks or punctures anywhere on the entire engine?

Check all work orders for service on the engine. You should determine the reasons for any major work performed, e.g., collision, wear and tear, accident, etc.

If you are not comfortable doing the following, then please have a qualified mechanic do the job:

Pull a **compression check** on all cylinders. The compression in each cylinder should be within a few pounds of the others, per the specs on the engine. Check plugs for proper gap and carbon build-up.

The engine's **lower unit** should be drained. Check for any water or metal particles, which are signs of major problems. Check the engine's **skeg** (the bottom-most part of an outboard engine, or outer unit of an I/O). If it is well worn, the engine has been bounced off the bottom some. Look at the propeller. Is it beaten up with a lot of dings and nicks? Do the blades look in reasonably good shape and aligned, considering its use and age?

Sometimes gouges, cuts, and heavy nicks on the skeg and propeller are indicators of a **bent propeller shaft.** Check for this by holding a ruler or pencil at the prop nut. Then, with the shifter in Neutral, spin the prop. Carefully observe it for any out-of-true rotation. The ruler is a good reference to indicate any prop wobble, which is symptomatic of a bent shaft.

CAUTION!

Make certain the engine's shifter really is in Neutral before you touch that prop, or you could lose some valuable body part.

Steering and engine controls should be checked for feel, function, and freedom of motion. They should operate smoothly and the things they control should respond positively.

The engine's **cooling system** must be checked for maintaining the proper power head temperatures within specified limits under all loads.

The **electrical system** should deliver the proper voltages and current flows throughout the boat. Alternator output should be within specified limits.

Incidentally, many folks enjoy working with the electrical system for troubleshooting and for the installation of accessories. This is fine, but there are certain standards that should be followed. So when you look over a boat, keep an eye out for bad wiring jobs. You can usually tell these by carelessly taped joints, tangles of wires jammed into nooks and cubby holes, flickering lights, radio static, fuse problems, and the like.

Installed electrical fixtures should be wired into **fuse blocks** or fused switch plates. Tapping directly into a lead from some other appliance, or directly into the boat's main power line, should not be attempted as it leads to corrosion and short circuits.

In outboard engines the proper fuel and oil ratio is critical. Most smaller (under 40 HP) two-cycle outboards use pre-mixed fuels. This is where the engine oil is added in specified proportion to an external or internal fuel tank. These tanks and fuel lines should be checked for condition and wear. Large, modern outboards utilize an external oil reservoir, with the oil mixed with the gasoline at some point prior to the fuel's flowing into the cylinders. As there have been serious problems with some of these oil delivery systems in the past, you should inquire about any problems with the engine you are evaluating.

Check all the **fuel lines.** Are all fittings tight and not leaking? Is there any smell of fuel? Are fuel hoses in good condition? Are there any signs of past fuel leaks? Are the fuel filters clean?

If installed, coolant **hoses** and **belts** must be checked for condition and age. You should feel each hose for hard or mushy spots, which indicate likely failure points. All belts should be carefully examined for wear and general condition. Look for frayed and brittle spots. If hoses and belts have been on the engine more than two years (less in extreme hot or cold conditions), they should be replaced.

The Used Trailer

Carefully inspect the trailer for any obvious defects. It should look well cared for. Check the trailer for rust and corrosion, particularly in the inside angles of trailer frame members. Check all welds for cracks.

Look at the **suspension system.** Boat trailers usually have leaf springs. If leaves are heavily rusted and flat, or sagging downward, the springs should be replaced. Good leaf springs should look black and be curved upward.

Check the trailer's **wheel bearings** and **seals.** There should be no leaking grease. Carefully check the inside of each wheel for rusty-appearing (brownish in color) grease thrown from the inside seals. This could indicate rusty bearings or races, and trouble. Are BEARING BUDDIES, or equivalent, installed?

Have the loaded rig run at highway speeds for about 10 miles, if at all possible. Then stop and carefully touch both wheel bearing housings. Remember, warm is OK. Hot is not. When you check the bearings, also feel the **trailer tires.** If they are hot, they've probably been run under-inflated in the past, and may need to be replaced. Is there excessive or uneven tread wear, cuts, gouges? Have the tires been sitting unprotected for months in the hot sun, ice, or snow? Are there any sidewall cracks?

Is there a usable **spare trailer tire,** of the correct size, mounted on the trailer? Can *you* get that spare off its carrier easily? Are any special tools needed?

Does the **winch** work smoothly and easily? Is the winch cable or strap in sound condition?

Is the **coupler** mounted solid and true on the trailer tongue? Will it fit the ball on your tow vehicle?

Are there **safety chains** that fit your tow vehicle?

Is the trailer's electrical wiring intact and sound? Do *all* the lights work? Try them on your tow vehicle to be sure.

Is there any untreated corrosion anywhere on the trailer?

In some states, boat trailers have to be inspected on a regular basis. If that is the case in your state, check with the seller to make sure that he has had a proper inspection performed. If this isn't done prior to closing, you'll have to pay later for the inspection, plus maybe a fine, and possibly for some repairs to make the trailer roadworthy.

Decision Time

If you note things wrong with the rig at this point, you have to decide whether to abort that deal, or use the noted defects as bargaining chips in your negotiations. If the defects are minor, we recommend going ahead if you really like the rig.

> *Any used rig you are seriously considering should be inspected by a qualified marine technician, to include an on-water check. The cost of all this is relatively low, and the dollars you save could be significant.*

If the technician says all is well, you and the seller, or the seller's agent, should take a test ride in the boat. Do not operate the boat without the seller being there with you.

Take the helm and run the boat in calm water through the engine's entire RPM range. How does it run and sound? Does it have enough power to make it go the way you like? Does the engine respond well to throttle changes, or is it rough or sluggish? Does the throttle move smoothly and positively through its entire range?

Does the steering feel firm and tight? Does the boat turn cleanly and positively?

Can you see well while seated at the helm, or do you have to stand up, or sit on the back of the seat to see all around the boat? Do you feel completely in control at all times?

Now try the boat in moderate wave conditions at medium speed. How does she ride and handle in the waves? Note that the boat should feel stable while underway. It may pitch, roll, and yaw some, but there should be a feeling of complete control at the helm.

Try some turns in various wave conditions at various speeds. How does she ride and feel in the turns? Does she soak you with spray, or does she ride dry? Do you feel comfortable and confident while underway in the waves? If not, why not?

Run her at low speeds, going forward, both in calm water and moderate waves. Does she respond to the helm positively? Put her in Reverse and try straight backing and then various turns. Does she take the helm well while backing? Would you feel confident taking her through some crowded marina on a windy Saturday afternoon?

A boat must feel right to you during the test ride to continue the negotiations. If you just aren't sure, say good-bye to that deal and look elsewhere. There are plenty of other boats around. It may take a little more time to find just what you want, but it sure beats paying a lot of bucks for a rig in which you and yours just don't feel completely comfortable.

Closing the Deal

If the complete rig has functioned to your satisfaction, you are now in a position to make the seller an offer, and possibly close the deal. Here's where your horse trading skills will prove handy.

Remember, you should never pay the seller's asking price unless you are contributing to his charity or retirement fund. You might make your initial offer around one-half of what the seller asks. This may bring some snorts and laughter, but may-be not. Give it a shot. You might just luck out, particularly toward the end of the year, or if there are some problems with the rig.

If there *are* problems with the rig, you may have a chance for an outstanding deal. Remember, some of the very best deals can come out of major price reductions you negotiate because of noted problems. A smart buyer can play even a relatively minor defect into a Titanic-sized situation with artful talk. This is particularly so if the seller really needs to sell the rig, and is not all that knowledgeable about the boat.

Most boat deals are easily negotiated if the seller really wants to sell, and you, the buyer, really want to buy. This may sound basic, but there are boat owners around who occasionally test the market without any real intention to sell. These people will take you down to the home stretch and back out. Your deal then collapses. Try to make sure you have a real seller as early as possible to avoid a lot of wasted time and effort.

There's **seller psychology** at work here that you should consider. This guy probably wants to sell his boat *now*. He wants out and quick. He's tired of pouring money into the thing and thinks you are a live buyer with cash in hand. If you encourage that impression, he will probably take any reasonable offer, or maybe even an unreasonable one, if he's really hard-up, your timing is right, and you talk sweet enough.

When all the dealing is done and an agreement is reached with the seller, it is important that the terms of your deal be put in writing. The best way of doing this is by a **Bill of Sale**, or **Contract of Sale.** You should check with your lawyer or a boat dealer about this. In many states a simple form, available at most office supply companies, is adequate.

You should also inquire at your **State Boating Office** to see if there is any transfer fee in connection with the sale. In some states, boat trailers, engines, and boats are separately titled, and fees must be paid to the state upon transfer of these items from one citizen to another. It is important to find out about the situation in your state to avoid unpleasant surprises.

Selling Your Boat Rig

When the time finally comes and you're ready to part with your Pride and Joy, there are several things that you must do to make the sale go well. Now you change places from that of a buyer to seller. But when you flip-flop your viewpoint, you'll have an immediate leg-up, as you've already looked at a deal from the buyer's standpoint.

There are any number of ways to sell your boat. Witness the large number of classified ads in the papers every day. There are "boat trader" magazines in most parts of the country, ads on supermarket bulletin boards, at marinas, almost anywhere around boating areas. All of these are fine, but there's an easier way.

> *We recommend instead of selling the boat yourself, you contact your boat dealership, or a boat broker, and have them sell it for you on a consignment basis.*

Most dealers I know will be happy to take a consignment sale for a percentage of the gross. Ten percent is about the norm. For this the dealer will handle all the details of the sale. He'll advertise and show your boat, give on-water demonstrations, and finally close on the deal. This method seems the best for most busy people.

You will then, of course, miss the joys of face-to-face negotiations, showing the boat at all hours, and the on-water demos to a wide variety of the curious, insolvent folks who hanker for a Sunday afternoon boat ride.

But whichever way you decide to go, make sure that your boat, engine, and trailer are all working properly, unless you choose to disclose all the problems to prospective buyers, and adjust your selling price accordingly.

Have your rig super-clean when you try to sell. The time and effort to get everything shining is well worth it. The cleaner it is, the faster it sells!

Clearly identify and tag all items that go with the deal. For example, life jackets, boat covers, paddles, anchors, line, water skis, etc. It is bad business and deal-killing to show a boat with a lot of the extras on board, and then arrive at closing with an empty hull.

You should have available the work orders for all maintenance and other services performed, including the installation of any equipment on the boat, engine, and trailer. If you installed any items yourself, you should have the purchase invoices for the items.

Pricing your rig correctly is very important. Pricing too low makes people think something is wrong, when there is nothing wrong at all. Pricing too high will result in few, if any, interested buyers. You probably will not get back all that you have put into your rig, either in terms of things you've bought for the boat, or your sweat equity. Try, by all means, but don't be too disappointed when you fail. Complete recapture of your investment is usually not possible in any sort of normal market condition. Most dealers have copies of BUC Books and will be glad to help you set a fair price if you contract with them for the sale. Remember, they must actually see the rig before a price can be provided.

On a consignment sale, the dealer will normally charge you a one-time fee to inspect your boat, and tell you what needs to be done to sell it best. Most minor items you should be able to do yourself, but if you wish, the dealer will usually be pleased to make the necessary make-ready repairs to your rig for a small fee. Selling a boat can take some time. It is dependent on a variety of factors. Time of year is usually important, as is the general state of the economy where you live.

If you place your boat with a reputable dealer for a consignment sale, you are probably getting the percentages on your side for a more satisfying and faster transaction than if you try to sell it yourself.

True Costs of Boat Ownership

To avoid a lot of accounting gobbledegook, all costs here are either **Direct Costs** or **Indirect Costs.** We throw in a few comments here about the cost categories to provide other perspectives. You fill in the actual dollars for your individual case. We suggest using your estimated **cost per year** as your basis.

"Direct" means you've got to actually pay up either when the bill comes in or when the service and/or materials are purchased.

"Indirect" means you don't have to fork over any cash right now, but the costs will be realized in some way at some other time.

Direct Costs

1. Fuel and oil: $_____

You probably will be using the high octane fuel in accordance with your engine manufacturer's service instructions. Ask your boat dealer about this. You'll usually save bucks if you buy gasoline from regular service stations rather than shore-side marine service facilities.

You might find it cheaper to buy your engine oil in bulk from local marine service shops, but you must bring the container. Make sure you buy the right type for your engine.

2. Maintenance: $_____

This is for the labor and materials it costs you to keep your boat rig running. It is either "preventive" or "breakdown" maintenance. Remember, if you don't take care of your rig with preventive service *now,* it will take care of you *later.* When "later" comes, it usually involves a need for emergency services to drag you in from way out there on the water.

Although you can do a lot of the light maintenance work yourself, professional help will be required for many jobs. We strongly recommend that you select and utilize a quality marine service facility. Deal with them regularly. Pay your bills when due. Be square with them at all times and your boating pleasures will be significantly increased.

3. Boat Improvements: $_____

We've never known anyone who has purchased a boat and not added, or done something to it. Recognize this happy expenditure and include it in your budget.

4. Storage: $_____

Sometimes you've got to keep your rig some-place besides your driveway. If you decide to keep your boat in a commercial facility, always negotiate the fees. For example, if you sign a lease, you probably can get major savings if you pay for the entire lease period in advance. Also, if you lease a slip or a mooring, or use a stacking facility, ask to store your trailer on the premises free of charge.

5. Insurance: $_____

Insurance on your entire rig is an absolute must. It's important that you shop around for your marine insurance. Look in the Yellow Pages for insurance brokers.

6. Boat Registration: $_____

Almost every state has a recreational boat registration fee of some sort. The exact cost can be determined by calling your State Boating Office.

7. Trailer Registration: $_____

As boat trailers are "vehicles" the registration fee is normally paid through the same agency that handles motor vehicle licenses in your state.

8. Property Taxes: $_____

These taxes are levied in certain states. You should contact your local tax collecting agency to find out the amount levied on your rig.

9. Interest on Loan: $_____

If you are purchasing your boating rig by means of a loan from a financial institution, you should include the loan interest, and other loan charges, as a direct expense.

TOTAL DIRECT COSTS: $_____

Indirect Costs

10. Depreciation: $_____

This is the regular decrease in value of the boat, engine, and trailer over a period of time. When you sell your boat for less than it cost you, the difference between how much you got for the boat, and how much you paid for it, is the amount it depreciated.

11. Value Lost: $_____

This is the amount of interest you didn't earn on the total capital amount you have invested in your rig. Say you had taken the money that you now have in your rig and invested it in a Certificate of Deposit. The interest that CD would have paid you is the "Value Lost" of your rig.

TOTAL INDIRECT COSTS: $_____

GRAND TOTAL: $_____

NOTES

NOTES

Chapter 2

~~~~~~

Equipping the Boat—For Comfort and Safety

> *This chapter tells you how to properly equip your boat for maximum enjoyment.*

The equipping part can get mighty confusing sometimes. There seems to be a limitless amount of gear available to either hang on, or put in, your boat. Walk around any well stocked **chandlery** (a store where nautical gear is sold), or any large boat dealership, or peruse the boating catalogs that come in the mail, and you'll see stuff for boats that you never dreamed existed!

This chapter will help you get a handle on the situation. There are three sections that cover the main categories of equipment needed aboard your recreational power boat:

⚓ **Personal Boating Gear** tells about those personal things important for your comfort and enjoyment.

⚓ **Gear for Your Boat** discusses the basic things important for the pleasant and efficient operation of your vessel.

⚓ **Federally Required Equipment** describes the equipment that Federal regulations mandate be aboard your boat.

The items we tell you about here should be considered the minimum you need for safety and comfort. You will, we're sure, include many other items as time goes by. In fact, during the first couple of years after getting a boat, most of us buy a lot of the really neat boat things that look so good in the catalogs, or at the dealers. This is gear we simply have to have to make our boat the very best. Most of that stuff, however, soon gets retired to the back of the garage, or the trash can, after a few uses.

Personal Boating Gear

When you board a power boat there are certain personal items you'll need. Here are what seem to work best for many people.

Have and use good quality **sunglasses.** The glare off sunlit water can be fierce. Please don't use those cheap plastic throwaways you buy off a rack someplace. Instead, ask your eye doctor to recommend a high quality model to properly protect your eyes. Medium-grey polaroids are particularly good for fishing, incidentally.

Whenever you wear sunglasses (or your regular glasses, for that matter) on or around any boat, use one of those **keeper cords** that go around your neck and connect to the side pieces of the glasses. Then when the glasses fall off, they won't go much further than your chin.

You'll need a **visored cap** to keep the sun off your bald spot, and out of your eyes. Full-brimmed hats are also good because they protect your neck, and we all know that's important.

Wear comfortable clothes that you don't mind getting wet. If it's cold out there, dressing in layers helps. A lightweight, wind-and-water-resistant outer shell jacket is great, with whatever it takes to stay warm underneath. In any season, carry, or wear, a long-sleeved shirt to protect your arms against the sun, or cold, or insects. Your extra clothes carried aboard are best kept in a plastic bag to keep them reasonably dry.

The correct dressing for really heavy weather depends upon where you'll be doing your boating, and the time of year. If you have any doubts, ask some knowledgeable soul to suggest the right kind of **foul-weather clothes** for your local conditions. This is not a matter of vanity. The right clothes are important. In fact, they can be lifesaving, particularly if you're likely to be exposed to cold water or weather.

Wear **rubber-soled shoes** aboard the boat. Don't go barefoot, unless that's the way you usually dress, as you will ding your toes. Please don't wear leather-soled shoes, as they get very slippery, cause bad falls, and damage decks.

Use a high factor **sunscreen** cream, or lotion, on all ex-posed skin and keep re-applying it regularly. Ask your doctor which is best for your marine environment. We used to think that all this hue and cry about the dangers of the sun was the usual media hogwash trying to fill newspaper and air time on slow days. Then one fine day one of our fishing friends showed up with most of one side of his face bandaged. He had just had a number of facial growths hacked off. Doc told him it was the result of too many unprotected years of sun.

So play it smart. Use that sunscreen and wear a good hat.

While you're at Doc's, ask him about **motion sickness** remedies, if that's a problem. If you take any medication, make sure you have an adequate supply safely stowed in waterproof container(s) on your person before you board.

Make sure your **car keys,** and other items that you treasure, are safely stowed where they can't fall overboard.

Keep your regularly used **boat keys** on a **floating key holder.** Get two other complete back-up sets of your boat keys made. Keep one spare set stashed in your tow vehicle, and the other set with your regular car keys. We bet you'll need one or the other of these spare keys about once a month.

Now you may think all this doesn't apply to you, but it does. You'll lose gear at times and in ways you least expect. If you haul out your handkerchief to mop your fevered brow, your car keys will fly over the side. If you bend over the rail to net that big fish, and your brand new sunglasses will leave for **Davy Jones' Locker.** Wallets in the back pocket of your jeans are sure goners unless you button that pocket. Hand tools are notorious for slipping out of your sweaty hands into the drink. The list goes on and on.

Gear for Your Boat

These are the basic items you would normally have on a recreational power boat operating on inland and coastal waters. This list, of course, is not necessarily complete, as each Skipper has his own ideas and budget.

The Magnetic Compass

The marine magnetic compass dates back to our earliest seafaring ancestors. The basic concept is that a magnetized needle aligns itself with the Earth's magnetic field. Modern compasses are of two types: the **dome,** or front-reading card, and the **dish,** or back-reading card. Most small power boats use the dome type, but either is fine, depending on your personal preference.

The size of the compass card is a factor. Experience has shown that you should get the largest compass that the mounting space aboard your boat, and your budget, can handle.

There are several types of compass mountings. The **binnacle mount** is a separate stand or platform for the compass at the helm station. The **flush-mounted** compass is in a hole cut in some flat part of the helm station. In **bulkhead mounts,** the compass is placed in a hole cut in a bulkhead, which is any transverse wall in the hull. The **bracket mount** is very common, and allows the compass to be removed from the boat when not in use.

The compass should be located on, or very near, the vessel's centerline, where you can see it easily while at the helm.

After the compass is installed on the boat, you should get out on the water some quiet day and adjust it to point properly for your boat. Just follow the simple directions that come with the instrument. If there is a question, see your boat dealer.

Now learn how to effectively *use* that compass. Take a short course, get a good book, or check out an instructional video. Once you understand the basics, your navigation will be a lot easier and safer.

Boarding Ladder

We strongly recommend that all power boats be equipped with a **portable boarding ladder,** or an **installed transom ladder,** to assist in the recovery of overboard persons.

Mooring Lines

You need these so you can tie up and secure your boat when you pull into a dock or pier. Their length and diameter are determined by how and where you use your boat. As a general rule, you need a separate line for the bow and stern. There should be enough mooring line to enable the boat to move with the waves, swells, and tide.

We have found it convenient to keep four 25-foot, ½-inch diameter, braided nylon lines, each normally secured to the starboard and port cleats on the bow and stern on our 20-footer. This boat is operated in both fresh and salt water and these lines serve well.

Spring lines are dock lines that are extremely useful in docking and undocking your boat in close quarters, or in other conditions where her movements must be completely controlled. Secured to the bow cleat (forward spring), and a stern cleat (after spring), these lines are made fast on the pier or dock and the boat maneuvered off them while under power. Their effective use takes a lesson or two, and some experience, but it's time well spent.

Fenders

You'll need these fore, aft, and amidships to protect your boat in docks, slips, and other places where you tie up. These must be individually sized for your boat. You usually need six fenders (three on each side-bow, stern, and amidships), each long and fat enough to keep your boat's hull from contacting whatever is alongside.

Bow Line

This line is to secure or tow your boat from its bow eye. Ours has a heavy galvanized snap hook on the end, which is on the bow eye as needed. The **"bitter end"** is the end of the line in the boat.

The bow line should not be long enough to reach the transom of your boat when it's on the bow eye,

*because one fine day your bow line will go over-
board while you are underway. If it's longer than
your boat's overall length, it may be chopped by the
propeller.*

If you have a metal hook on the overboard end, you will
experience the thrill of some expensive sounds as that hook
and your churning propeller come together.

Boat Tool Boxes

Get two tool boxes made of steel, with good, solid latches.
Keep very lightly coated with oil. WD-40 works great.
We've been through many plastic boxes over the years, and
they just weren't strong enough to be used on board. They
would eventually break, and gear would dump out all over
the wrong places. Steel boxes may rust some, and may not
look too swanky as they age, but they're tough and keep on
working.

In the first box we keep **basic tools** that have proven
really useful over the years. These include a set of box- and
open-end wrenches, a 10-inch adjustable wrench, claw ham-
mer, hacksaw, several sizes of Phillips and flathead screw-
drivers, vise-grip pliers, slip-jaw pliers, wire cutters, needle-
nose pliers, one of those combination "insulation stripper,
connector squeezer" tools, a cheap circuit continuity checker
(try Radio Shack), feeler gauges, and a complete socket
wrench set. Make sure you have a socket that fits the spark
plugs of your boat engine.

In the second steel box we keep **shop supplies.** These
include a set of new spark plugs for the boat engine, all
properly gapped. Duct tape, plastic electric tape, WD-40, a
tube of heavy marine grease, **MARINE-TEX,** a stick of
epoxy putty, tube of **GOOP,** several feet of insulated wire,
assorted solderless electrical connectors, small roll of soft

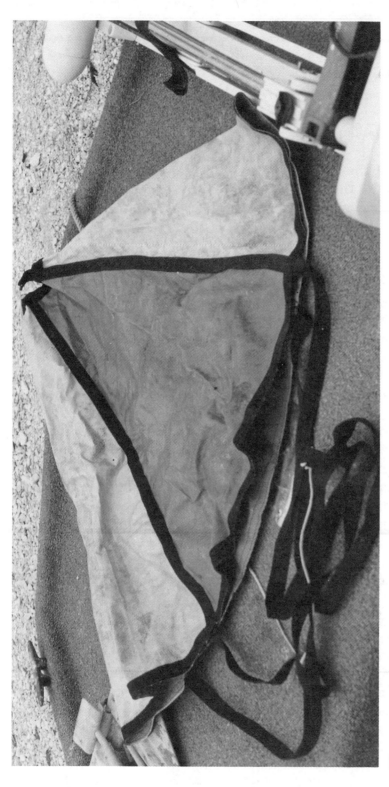

Figure 14. *Sea Anchor.* This is a collapsed sea anchor. It is about 4 feet in length and about 4 feet in diameter when open in the water. It is made of a very tough plasticized fabric. One-inch wide nylon straps comprise the rigging. When in use, the large end faces the boat. There is a "trip cord" to collapse the sea anchor when you pull it back into the boat.

wire, several spare fuses for every size needed on the boat, assorted stainless steel screws, washers, nuts and bolts, and a couple of old towels for spill wipe-ups.

Please buy first-quality "Made in America" tools and supplies. The imported tools that look so great in their blister packs just don't work out too well afloat. They seem to rust out quickly, and don't function as well. We recommend that you handle, heft, and carefully check each tool. Does it feel solid and well made? If it's a cutting tool, do the two cutting surfaces meet exactly?

We also recommend that you obtain the Shop Manuals for your engine, and for any other components on your vessel for which they are available. Your boat dealer should be able to get them for you. If not, write the manufacturer of the component. The cost is low and they'll save you a real bundle.

Spare Propeller

This can be an important get-home item, particularly if you are running an aluminum prop, as they ding easily. Remember, you should have the right tools and other gear on board to change out that prop while on the water, and know how to use them.

This is an easy job, but if you're new to boating please read your engine manual to get an idea of what to do. Then practice in shallow, warm, clear water with a hard bottom. You will quickly note how easy it is to drop things.

Sea Anchor

This is a canvas or floppy plastic cone, open at both ends. It is several feet in diameter at the large end. There is a rope or strap rigging at that larger end to connect to a line from your bow. It will help keep your vessel headed into the wind when your boat's engine is shut down. The amount of line you deploy depends on how strong the wind is blowing, and the size and type of boat you are operating. Ask for help on this from a local, experienced Skipper. The sea anchor is an important emergency item if you lose power while underway in bad weather.

A sea anchor is also useful if you're fishing and want to set up a "drift" across some promising water. Secure its rigging to an amidships cleat. When it's deployed, you'll ride downwind in a broached position, sideways to the wind. You may need two sea anchors, one at the bow and the other at the stern, to slow your drift if it's really windy. When you buy a sea anchor, get a good quality, heavy duty one, not the light plastic "drift" version. The heavy duty model costs more, but can save your hide on that stormy day when your engine dies.

Spot Lights

These may be either permanently mounted on your boat, or hand-held. Both types are connected to your boat's electrical system, unless you've got one of those hand-held rechargeable models. The rechargeable batteries, incidentally, are good for about 20 minutes' continuous burn at full charge.

We recommend that you get several of the best quality hand-held spotlights you can find. These things always seem to fail when you really need them, and it's good to have a back-up right there. A problem with some of the cheaper hand-helds is that the bulbs don't last long and their switches fail. Replacement bulbs cost pretty close to the whole unit, if you can find them. If the switch goes bad, the whole unit probably should be junked.

We have found that the 500,000 candle power hand-held units seem to last the longest, and give good illumination for most purposes.

You may want to also consider a permanently mounted spotlight on your boat. This is a simple installation for either you or your boat service facility. The downside of having an installed light is the theft and vandalism problem.

Flashlights

We keep several small flashlights around to give passengers when a night trip is planned. They make life a lot more pleasant for all concerned. Tell passengers not to point them around the helm, however, as that'll ruin the helmsman's night vision.

Anchor System

You need an anchor which, when properly in place on the bottom, will securely hold your boat under the worst conditions of wind, current, and tide. This is an important safety matter.

The proper anchor system for your particular boat depends on where you are operating your boat, and the prevailing weather and sea conditions. The "system" consists of the **anchor** itself, the **rode** (anchor line), the **anchor chain** (connects the anchor to the rode), and the connecting **shackles.**

Note that you may well need two complete anchor systems for your boat, depending on your operating location and conditions. Your dealer, other local boaters, your local Power Squadron, or the Coast Guard Auxiliary should be able to provide you guidance on this matter.

There are many anchors and all have their unique uses. The main types now on the market include the Danforth, Plow, Bruce, Kedge, Stock, Grapnel, Folding, and Mushroom. Rodes are made of either twisted nylon, braided synthetic, or manila material.

It is important that you have the right anchor system for your operating situation. For your specific applications please seek the advice of a qualified boat dealer, or the local Coast Guard station.

Water-Ski Bridle

This inexpensive item is useful in towing, not only water skiers, but also disabled small boats in light weather and water conditions. It connects to the two tow eyes on the stern panel of most trailer boats, and has a single **bight** (loop) to which you connect the tow line.

Extra Line

This is a matter of personal choice dependent upon how and where you use your boat. Over the years we've found that it's mighty useful to have an extra 200 feet of ½-inch twisted nylon line available on board.

Charts

The proper nautical charts for the ocean and coastal waters on which you operate provide an important safety dimension. They show the nature and shape of the coast, water depths, character of the bottom, prominent landmarks, port facilities, aids to navigation, marine hazards, and other pertinent information.

Nautical charts are regularly updated to aid in safe navigation. This updating information can be obtained from **"Local Notice to Mariners,"** published by the U.S. Coast Guard. The **National Ocean Service** produces a variety of charts and chart-related products that are available by mail from:

National Ocean Service
Distribution Branch, N/CG33
Riverdale, MD 20737

Send for a free catalog and get an idea of all the good items they publish.

Nautical charts are also available from retail sources (boat dealerships, sporting goods stores, etc.) in the areas where you operate. Keep aboard your boat charts for the waters you frequent. The cost is low, and the information presented can be invaluable.

First Aid Kit

You should have an adequate first aid kit on board. The size and type of kit you need is determined by how and where you use your boat. If you go on long cruises well away from civilization, you may need a much more extensive kit than if you're a day boater on some small lake or river.

We do not recommend that you buy an advertised "marine" first aid kit unless you are certain that it will fit your boating plans. You may find that off-the-shelf drug store kits, or kits you put together yourself, will do the job just as well, if not better. Contact your medical advisors, or your local fire department about this.

> *Make certain that your first aid kit is stored where it can't get wet. A tightly-lidded plastic TUPPERWARE container works fine.*

Bilge Pumps and Bailers

The electric bilge pump mounted in your bilge usually works fine. One day, though, it will conk out. Carrying a spare bilge pump is a good idea. They are relatively cheap, and very easily installed. There are also hand-operated bilge pumps available from your boat dealer, or by mail. It would pay you to have one or two of those aboard if you venture away from shore at all.

We also recommend your having a bucket or two aboard your boat. You may think you'll never need them, but there will come a time. We keep a couple of collapsible canvas buckets aboard, and they work great for a variety of water-hauling tasks.

Boat Hook / Push Poles / Paddle

You need something to shove your boat around, or to reach out and grab something when you're coming on and off the beach, dock, or mooring. We've been using a telescoping push pole with a "Y" shaped wooden foot for some time, and it works fine.

Fuel and Oil

Several knowledgeable folks have told us that you need to have aboard one-third of your fuel to get there, one-third to get back, and one third in reserve. Along with this, you should have spare engine oil. This makes sense, but please check this out for where and how *you* operate. You may need a lot more, or less, of that precious stuff.

Batteries

This is applicable to those with boats that utilize battery power to crank their engines, and run the onboard electronic and electrical accessories. That would probably include almost everybody, except those of you with really small outboards.

Some time ago we got stuck way out on the water at sundown, in lowering weather, without enough fire in the battery to crank the engine. We had been running a VHF radio, an AM/FM radio, and a fishfinder, all the while trolling with the big engine ticking over at very low RPM. The alternator apparently wasn't putting out enough to adequately recharge the one battery. This could have been a bad situation, because the VHF radio was also kaput with that low battery. We got out of there with no real problem thanks to the help of a passing fisherman, but decided that there must be a better way.

After considering the total loads on the electrical system, we installed two batteries in the boat, with a four-position master switch (Off, Battery 1, Battery 2, Both). The two batteries installed were the heaviest **Group 27 batteries,** with **gel electrolyte,** we could find. They are kept charged with the boat's engine while underway at cruise speeds, and with a **shoreside battery charger** as needed. This arrangement works fine, and we have had adequate power since. As an additional benefit, that master switch provides another level of security for the boat.

Drinking Water

> *"Water, water, everywhere, and not a drop to drink"*
>
> (Samuel Coleridge, "Rime of the Ancient Mariner")

That could be you out there, thirsting away, unless you fill your water tank, or pack a jug, or canteens, with some good fresh water for you, your passengers, and your dog. It's even good to do this on most bodies of fresh water, because of the pollution. Make sure the container tops are tightly screwed down before you stow them. If you don't, you know what will happen.

Survival Gear

Almost every Skipper has some form of survival gear on board. It may be as simple as extra clothing, or one of those **MYLAR "space age" blankets,** with perhaps a **propane heater** or **lamp.** It may be quite elaborate, with a full range of cold-weather survival gear, a fully equipped life raft, distilled-water maker, firearms, plus sophisticated electronic rescue equipment. It all depends on what you feel you need, how much space you have to stow the gear, and how much you can afford to spend.

You have to address the "what could happen" factors as realistically as possible, and equip your boat accordingly. Don't fail to address this matter, because when you need that survival gear you'll need it real bad.

Let's now discuss electronic devices that are useful on many power boats. Major advances in solid-state electronics in recent years have introduced a whole line of reallunique and reliable marine devices. The booming recreational boating market has made these devices available at reasonable prices.

Fluxgate Compass

Instead of using a compass card reacting to the Earth's magnetic field, the fluxgate compass uses a stationary electronic sensor on the boat. As your vessel moves, the orientation of the sensor changes with respect to the Earth's magnetic field. Small voltages are then generated by the sensor and are read hundreds of times per second by a microcomputer in the instrument.

The microcomputer continuously averages these readings and portrays them on a screen. The operator sees an electronic portrayal of the vessel's heading in either the shape of a compass face or in digital form. Direct interface with LORAN, GPS, your autopilot, and other equipment is easily possible.

Speedometer/SUM LOG

This instrument will keep track of mileage covered, and give you an accurate measurement of speed at any time while underway. This can be very useful in the **Dead Reckoning** navigation, a method whereby en route speeds, distances, and times are computed by the simple formula, Distance = Rate × Time.

Fuel Flow Meter

This gives a rate of fuel consumption in gallons per hour. Some units will total the fuel consumed and display it in gallons. This information is very helpful on long trips in connection with your navigation calculations.

LORAN

Your **LO**ng **RA**nge **N**avigation unit can tell you where you are (latitude and longitude), your speed, course, time to destination, etc. Shore-based transmitting antennae are used, and a two-dimensional position fix is computed by a basic electronic triangulation method. This device is available as a hand-held, or on a fixed mount in your boat. A suitable antenna is required. LORAN is best used where the transmitted signals are of good quality and reliable. Many catalogs feature LORAN navigational receivers for well under $400.

Well-proven over many years, LORAN is useful for off-shore, coastal, and other big water navigation. It will, however, take you a while to learn to use LORAN to the fullest advantage. You must study the owner's manual carefully, and preferably get some formal instruction. Check with the nearest Coast Guard facility regarding the best use of this navigational aid in your operating area.

Global Positioning System (GPS)

This Department of Defense (DOD) sponsored, 24 satellite based technology, has been used in recent years with a high level of accuracy and reliability by the Armed Forces. It is found in many weapons systems, and aboard military land vehicles and aircraft. It is theoretically accurate to within 10 meters.

GPS (sometimes called "NavStar") provides non-military users a position fix rapidly and with a good degree of accuracy. It is more reliable than LORAN as it is not subject to most weather interferences. In the non-military mode, GPS is accurate within about 100 meters, 95 percent of the time. This is due to the use of a DOD signal degradation security program called Selective Ability.

The Coast Guard has advised that the **Differential GPS** is presently under development, with a 1996 completion date for all three coasts and the Great Lakes. This system should provide an accuracy of less than 20 meters, 95 percent of the time for non-military users in the continental United States. This system corrects the intentional errors introduced by the Selective Ability security program.

The GPS concept is really great. With minimal experience on a unit, you will indeed be amazed with the usefulness and convenience of this device, both on land and water. There are, though, many unanswered questions regarding the future of LORAN vis-a-vis GPS, due to Federal government budgetary constraints. These two taxpayer-supported systems provide users essentially the same basic thing: a position fix by latitude and longitude, and, in some GPS sets, the altitude of the receiving unit above the earth's surface. This matter should be resolved by 1996. GPS units are available in hand-held and fixed mount systems at prices under $500. Make certain you determine the antenna needs of any set you consider.

RADAR

Eight and 16-mile **Ra**dio **D**etection **A**nd **R**anging units are available at reasonable prices from local dealers and marine catalogs. These units have become very popular with many small boat Skippers operating in adverse conditions. RADAR will help you locate buoys, other boats, oil rigs, shoreline cities, etc. in poor visibility.

The skilled use of this 50-year-old-plus, well-proven technology will definitely enhance your safety while underway. With some training and practice you should find it easy to use, and a positive benefit for your boat if you operate during times of decreased visibility. Your RADAR becomes your eyes-in-the-fog. The development of much smaller RADAR antenna and LCD (liquid crystal diode) backlit screens has been a major improvement for many small boats.

Depth Recorders

There are many variations of this important navigational tool, from a simple depth indicator, to devices which show the type and structure of the bottom, and everything in between.

These devices all use downward-aimed cone(s) of energy from a transponder, located on the hull of the boat. The effective depth of the unit depends on the amount of power applied in generating the cone(s). Some units are accurate to well over 600 feet of water.

The transponder reads the echoes from the emitted signals, and passes the needed information to a microcomputer located in the body of the instrument. What the transponder "sees" is then portrayed on either a LCD screen or on moving graph paper. Recorders with LCD displays show a transitory look at what's below, while the graph unit gives a permanent picture you can put in your pocket.

VHF Radio

The **V**ery **H**igh **F**requency **marine radio** is a primary means of communication on most big waters. VHF range is about 20 miles boat-to-boat. Most Coast Guard stations are reachable at 20-50 miles. If you operate on big water, your boat should have an installed VHF radio with 25 watts of output power. This is a most important safety device, and you should get the best quality you can afford.

Your **VHF antenna** is critical. Up to a certain point, the longer antenna you have, the better. That point depends on how large a boat you are operating. The 8-foot fiberglass antenna is now very popular for many recreational power boats. Your antenna should be mounted as high on the vessel as possible to enable the longest possible range, as VHF are "line-of-sight" transmissions.

The antenna should be set up in a non-corrosive mount. The antenna and mount must be of the highest quality so that the corrosive environment, and the constant engine vibrations and motion of the boat, will not weaken them. The 12-volt power supply to the radio should be properly fused and be of at least 10-gauge wire to reduce power losses.

Hand-held VHF radios with 5W/1W output power are useful for short range situations. They should not be relied on as your sole communications capability. Their range is about 5 miles maximum, and their battery power supply always seems to run out quickly if used to any extent.

Be aware that as a non-commercial radio operator you are *not required* to possess an operator's license to use your VHF unless you are in foreign waters. You *do require* a ship license for your radio equipment. This license is not transferable and stays with that vessel as long as you own it. When you get a new boat you must also get a new license for the VHF radio you install.

EPIRB

The **E**mergency **P**osition **I**ndicating **R**adio **B**eacon is an important life saving device. The Class A and Class B EPIRB units are the most popular for recreational boaters operating off-shore, in coastal areas, and on the Great Lakes. Both transmit distress signals on 121.5 and 243.0 MHz. These frequencies are constantly monitored by military and civilian aircraft, Coast Guard Search and Rescue aircraft, and United States and Russian satellites.

The Class A turns itself on automatically in the water, while the Class B must be turned on manually. There is a Class C EPIRB which transmits an alert and locate beacon on VHF/FM channels; however, these Class C units are not recommended for off-shore use because of limited range. There is a relatively new class of EPIRB now in use aboard certain Federally-mandated vessels. These are Category I and II units. Although these transmit on 121.5 MHz, their primary beacon transmits on 406 MHz.

Category I and II units are now primarily used for far off-shore use, but some feel that one day they will be standard for all marine applications.

Register your 406 MHz EPIRB with:

NOAA/NESDIS
Federal Building No. 4
4401 Suitland Road
Suitland, MD 20746.

Call (301) 763-4680 to get a registration form, or to see if you are already registered by the dealer who sold you the unit(s).

Cellular Telephones

Investigate the cellular coverage in your home area, and any other areas where you plan to use your boat. We have used cellular quite successfully in the last year both on Gulf Coast waters, as well as on the large reservoirs here in the Southwest, and found it convenient and hassle-free.

You should be aware, however, that the Coast Guard can't get a **directional fix** on your position when you call them on your cellular telephone, as they can with the VHF.

Federally Required Equipment

The following items are Federally mandated for boats under 26 feet in length. These are minimal requirements. Please note that they do not guarantee the complete safety of the vessel, nor any level of comfort.

Navigation Lights

The U.S. Coast Guard Navigation Rules cover lighting requirements for every type of watercraft. These Rules

require that all recreational vessels must display navigation lights between sunset and sunrise and under other
periods of reduced visibility as follows:

> *"Boats less than 26 feet while underway must show
> a white light visible through 360 degrees to a dis-
> tance of at least 2 miles, plus red and green bow
> lights visible for at least 1 mile.*
>
> *Such boats while anchored must show a white 360-
> degree light from where it can best be seen on the
> boat to a distance of 2 miles."*

If you operate your boat at night without good lights
showing, you are asking for a violent death. Don't chance it,
as the risk doesn't make it worthwhile.

Backfire Flame Arrestor

One approved device is required on each carburetor of all
gasoline engines installed after April 25, 1940, except outboard motors.

Sound-Producing Devices

Every vessel less than 39.4 feet in length must carry a
sound-producing device which can be heard for at least
½ mile. That device can be a bell, whistle, or horn.

In addition to the installed electric horn on the
boat, we've been carrying a couple of those beer-can-size
compressed air horns. You can get about 30 honks out
of one charge of air. When empty, take it to almost
any gas station and recharge from their air hose. These
little horns put out a real blast. They are handy as
back-up when the installed boat horn doesn't work
properly.

Visual Distress Signals

These are required on **coastal waters,** which include the U.S. waters of the Great Lakes, territorial seas, and those waters connected directly to them, up to the point where the body of water is less than 2 miles wide.

Boats less than 16 feet must carry approved visual distress signals for night use.

Boats larger than 16 feet, and other boats carrying six or more for-hire passengers, must carry visual distress signals approved for both daytime and nighttime use.

Be aware that most flares, meteors, and other incendiary devices are dated and must be replaced upon expiration. This is an item that the Coast Guard folks almost always check during an inspection of your boat. Incidentally, don't throw your outdated devices away. Instead, keep them to back up the newer ones.

Day-Only Distress Signals

⚓ An orange flag with black disc and square; orange smoke signal that can be hand-held or floated on the water.

Day and Night Distress Signals

⚓ Hand-held red flare, or parachuted red meteor

Night Only Distress Signals

⚓ Electric light-producing devices.

Any combination of signal devices selected from the above types when carried in the number required may be used to meet both day and night requirements.

You will need a total of three of each type for day and night use.

We strongly recommend that you carry the approved distress-signal devices any time you operate your boat. It's very important that you be able to visually signal to others if you are having problems while afloat.

Ventilation

Good ventilation is important to clear enclosed spaces on your boat of flammable vapors. These can be extremely dangerous when ignited, causing explosions and catastrophic fire.

All vessels built after April 25, 1940 which use gasoline for electrical generation, mechanical power, or propulsion are required to be equipped with a ventilation system. As the provisions of the law can be confusing, we suggest that you refer ventilation questions to your dealer or the Coast Guard. However, if your boat bears a label containing the words "This boat complies with U.S. Coast Guard safety standards," you can assume that the design of your boat's ventilation system satisfies the regulations.

Fire Extinguishers

At least one B-I type Coast Guard-approved hand-portable extinguisher is required on boats less than 26 feet.

Fire extinguishers are not required by Federal regulations on outboard motor boats under 26 feet, and on boats not carrying passengers for hire, if the construction of such motorboat will not permit the entrapment of explosive or flammable gases or vapors, and if the fuel tanks are not permanently installed.

We recommend, however, that at least one Coast Guard-approved fire extinguisher be carried aboard every boat at all times.

There may be some things worse than a fire on board a boat while underway, but not very many. If a fire starts, you want to be able to extinguish it right then.

So carry the right type extinguishers of the best quality and in perfect operating condition.

Check your extinguishers at least monthly to make sure the seals and tamper indicators are intact, and that the pressure gauge shows a good reading. Make sure the bottle isn't obviously damaged, corroded, leaking, or has clogged nozzles. If something is wrong with the bottle, either fix it right then, or get a new one.

Make sure your extinguishers are mounted in a convenient spot so you can get at them instantly.

Don't stow them in a locker or bag, or stash them away in some easily forgotten location. When you need a fire extinguisher, you're going to need it right then and there. There will be no time to be fishing around in the bottom of some locker trying to find the thing.

The following will give you useful information about fire extinguishers:

The "A" designation is for "flammable materials," while the "C" is for "electrical" fires. The "B" designation indicates that the fire extinguishers are designed to put out flammable liquid fires.

All type B-I extinguishers can be used aboard your boat. We do not, however, recommend using a foam extinguisher in the interior of a boat unless absolutely necessary. This is due to the difficulty in cleaning up the residue after use. Foam makes a real mess inside. The Halon Vapor and Carbon Dioxide extinguishers are effective, and leave no residue. The Dry Chemical devices are also effective, but they deposit a fine white powder in areas where used.

Here are some facts about the B-I extinguisher used in boats less than 26 feet. They can contain any one of the following:

Foam	1.25 gallons
CO_2	4.00 pounds
Dry Chemical	2.00 pounds
Halon Vapor	2.50 pounds

The B-II extinguisher is used on boats 26 feet and larger, and contains more of the same fire suppressants as the B-I.

We recommend you seek additional information about marine fire extinguishers from either the Coast Guard, your boat dealer, or your local fire department.

Personal Flotation Device (PFD)

PFDs must be Coast Guard-approved, in good and service-able condition, and of the appropriate size for the intended user. They must be readily accessible. They should not be stowed in duffel bags, in locked or closed compartments, or under other gear.

According to the **Coast Guard,** the most common causes of boating deaths are drowning and hypothermia. Both are conditions where the victims might have survived had they been wearing the proper PFD. Everyone should wear a PFD at all times if conditions become hazardous, and always in cold weather. The Coast Guard recommends that PFDs should be worn at all times by children and non-swimmers.

Cold water can be a particular hazard. Persons not wearing a PFD can be rapidly overcome and drown quickly unless immediately rescued. A properly fitted, brightly colored PFD can be of great assistance in such a rescue.

Note that in many states children under 12 years of age are required to wear an appropriate PFD at all times when in a launched boat. Please check with your **State Boating Office.**

Now let's look at the several types of PFD.

The **TYPE I PFD, OFF-SHORE LIFE JACKET** provides the most buoyancy. It is effective for all waters, especially open, rough, or remote waters where rescue may be delayed. It is designed to turn most unconscious wearers in the water to a face-up position. The Type I comes in adult and child sizes.

Advantages: Excellent performance
Disadvantages: Very bulky and cumbersome, may be uncomfortable out of the water

The **TYPE II PFD, NEAR-SHORE BUOYANT VEST** is intended for calm, inland waters, where there is a good chance of quick rescue. This type will not turn unconscious wearers face-up in the water. The Type II comes in three sizes—adult, medium child, and small child.

Advantages: Good flotation and low cost
Disadvantages: May be uncomfortable, not suitable for rough or cold water

The **TYPE III PFD, FLOTATION AID** is good for calm, inland water, or where there is a good chance of quick rescue. It is designed so wearers can place themselves in a face-up position in the water. It has the same essential buoyancy as the Type II PFD.

Advantages: Most comfortable for continuous wear; comes in many styles, colors, and sizes. Allows wearer to swim. Useful in the many water sports
Disadvantages: Not suitable for rough or cold water

The **TYPE IV PFD, THROWABLE DEVICE** is intended for calm, inland water with heavy boat traffic, where help is always present. It is not designed to be worn, but to be thrown to a person in the water. Type IV devices include buoyant cushions, ring buoys, and horseshoe buoys.

> *Advantages:* Low cost and easily throwable
> *Disadvantages:* Persons must be able to grasp and hang on to this PFD while in the water. This may render it unsuitable for injured or disabled persons.

The **TYPE V HYBRID INFLATABLE PFD** is the least bulky of all PFD types. The Hybrid is a cross between purely inflatable devices, and conventional PFDs with flotation material. The Hybrid contains a small amount of flotation material, plus a chamber which can be inflated by mouth, by carbon dioxide cartridge, or by other mechanical means. Performance is equal to a Type I, II, or III PFD when inflated. The Hybrid PFD must be worn at all times while underway, unless the wearer is below decks, or in an enclosed space.

> *Advantages:* Very comfortable and stylish; may provide better flotation than Types II and III.
> *Disadvantages:* Expensive; requires attentive maintenance; cannot be used for persons weighing less than 90 pounds because some persons may not be able to quickly inflate the device in an emergency situation

The **TYPE V, SPECIAL USE DEVICE** is intended for specific activities. It may be carried aboard instead of another PFD only if used according to the Coast Guard-approved conditions on the label. Some Type V devices provide significant hypothermia protection. Varieties include deck suits, work vests, and several models of the on-board sailing vest.

Remember that:

Boats less than 16 feet must be equipped with one Type I, II, III, IV, or V PFD for each person aboard.

Boats 16 feet or longer must be equipped with a Type I, II, III, or V, PFD for each person aboard, plus at least one Type IV must be available to be thrown to persons in the water.

Type V PFDs have restrictions marked on them which must be observed. If a Type V PFD is to be counted toward the minimum requirements, it must actually be worn.

*A person on **water skis** is considered on board your vessel, and requires a PFD for Coast Guard compliance purposes.*

It is certainly advisable for all water skiers to wear a PFD designed to withstand impact with the water at high speed. "Impact Class" marking on PFD labels refers to PFD strength, not personal protection. Check your state law on water skiers, as there are variances among the jurisdictions.

She starts—she moves—she seems to feel
The thrill of life along her keel!

Longfellow, *The Building of the Ship*

NOTES

NOTES

Chapter 3

~~~~~~

Trailering—Maneuver with Confidence

> *This chapter helps rid you of those feelings*
> *that hauling a boat around on a trailer*
> *is one of life's lesser joys!*

Open road problems usually occur when something breaks or malfunctions on the trailer. You can often see these unhappy boaters alongside almost any road leading to a weekend waterway. Their boats are pointing at strange angles, and there's usually a wheel flat on the ground and an axle in the mud.

Launch ramp angst is usually felt in direct proportion to the number of other boaters using the facility, and your trailering skill level. Throw in a slick ramp, a hot day, several inexperienced boaters, a drunk or two, and things hit the skids in a hurry. Tempers flare. Ugly words, glares, and gestures are exchanged. All the fun of boating evaporates. You're left with a sour taste that lasts the whole trip. Sound familiar?

After a lifetime of hauling boats around we want to share with you some great ideas that will help you avoid a lot of grief. We'll talk about **Your Tow Vehicle, Handling Your Rig, Getting Ready, On the Road,** and **Launching and Recovering.**

Your Tow Vehicle

Whether it's the family sedan, a pickup truck, or one of the many sport utility vehicles wheeling around, your tow vehicle must have enough power to *effortlessly* pull your fully loaded rig.

Most full-size boat trailers need a tow vehicle with a **heavy-duty engine,** preferably an eight cylinder, or big six, for adequate power. If you don't have an eight or big six, you may still be OK, provided that you don't have a really heavy boat, many hills, rough roads, or steep launch ramps to negotiate. Please check with a vehicle dealer or service facility if you have any doubts about the adequacy of your tow vehicle.

When you see that dealer you should know the **total weight of your trailer,** boat, and the gear you normally carry. This would include all boat fuel, and water, if you plan to fill those tanks before you begin your road trip.

That total weight should be less than the **Gross Vehicle Weight Rating (GVWR)** of your trailer, as shown on its **Capacity Plate.** This is located on the left forward side of the trailer frame.

If you aren't sure about your total weight, have your loaded trailer weighed at a truck weigh station, lumber yard, feed store, or wherever they have vehicle weigh scales.

If you overload the trailer, your tow vehicle will have problems on hills, with passing, and any time full engine power is required. There also could be serious structural problems with the trailer.

If you underload the trailer, a dangerous situation called **"fishtailing"** may arise. This is due to the insufficient weight on the tow vehicle hitch.

It is important that 5 to 10 percent of the total weight of the trailer be applied to the tow vehicle hitch by the trailer coupler.

If there is not enough weight on the tow vehicle hitch from the trailer coupler, you should move the load being carried in the boat forward. If that doesn't solve the problem, see your boat or trailer dealer. Incidentally, you can use a bathroom scale to check the weight on the coupler on most boat trailers.

Tow Vehicle Questions

Get the answers to these from your vehicle dealer as necessary:

⚓ Is your engine sufficiently powerful to handle the load?

⚓ Does it require an **oil cooler** and/or **oversized radiator?**

⚓ Is the transmission able to handle the increased loads? Does it require a **transmission cooler?**

⚓ Do the rear springs and shock absorbers need to be replaced with heavy-duty units?

⚓ Will you need a **limited-slip rear axle?**

⚓ Are the tow vehicle's **brakes** adequate to safely handle your loaded trailer?

⚓ Do you need to have brakes on your boat trailer to safely handle the total load?

Tow Vehicle Equipment

Here's what you need on your tow vehicle so you can safely and legally haul that boat trailer:

A high quality **tow hitch,** properly secured to the tow vehicle, is essential. The hitch must be either bolted or welded to the tow vehicle's frame. Simple bolting of the hitch to the rear bumper should not be attempted, unless the bumper is specially designed for trailer towing.

Ball hitches are commonly used for trailer towing. They come in several sizes depending on the load to be hauled. The size of the ball, and its allowable gross trailer weights, are usually stamped somewhere on the hitch. It is important that the right size hitch be installed for the total load to be towed, and that the trailer coupler matches the ball hitch exactly.

Hitches are rated as Class I through IV, the rating being dependent upon the total tongue weight of the fully loaded trailer. No more than about 10 percent of the trailer's gross vehicle weight should be on the hitch. Load equalizer hitches are used for heavier loads.

In those cases where the heights of the tow vehicle and trailer are substantially different, it is necessary to adjust the height of the hitch. This can be accomplished by using an under-vehicle **receiver.** This has a square, or rectangular, cross section, and "receives" the mount on which the **coupler ball** is secured. When in use, the ball mount is secured inside the receiver by a pull pin and clip. Note that the use of the receiver also enables the same tow vehicle to haul a variety of trailers by using different heights and sizes of ball mounts.

Under some conditions, it may be desirable to install another ball hitch on the front bumper of the tow vehicle. This **front bumper hitch** provides great maneuverability in crowded parking lots and slick ramps.

Large mirrors on both sides of your tow vehicle make trailering your boat a lot easier. If you are hauling a large boat that blocks your rear visibility, you should investigate installing the special mirrors used by truckers moving wide loads.

We suggest you install **fold-back mirrors,** in any case, so you can get into your garage with that tow vehicle.

Your tow vehicle must have the proper wiring circuitry to allow the tow vehicle's line current to flow into the trailer's circuit. Most auto parts shops sell a simple kit for this. This kit has the necessary wiring and the connectors to easily tie into your tow vehicle's wiring system.

We recommend that you install a fuse between the trailer and tow vehicle's circuits. In that way a short circuit in the trailer's wiring system won't blow a fuse in the tow vehicle.

While you're talking to your vehicle dealer, ask him to install a **heavy-duty turn signal flasher.** This will increase the intensity of the trailer's turn signals.

The above items are important to equip your tow vehicle for the most efficient handling of a loaded boat trailer. The total cost is relatively small compared to the total cost of your complete rig. The dollars spent here will be repaid many times over through the more pleasant and trouble-free operation of your tow vehicle.

IMPORTANT

If you are planning to use a vehicle still under warranty, make sure that the warranty is not voided by towing a trailer. Also check with your vehicle insurance carrier to make certain that you are properly covered when towing a boat trailer.

Handling Your Rig

Competent handling of a trailer boat rig is a learned skill. There's no magic to it. While you can master it by yourself, the best way is with a qualified person.

Forward towing is easy once you get the hang of how the rig feels, and you get used to seeing that boat behind you. **Backing** is more difficult, as that trailer doesn't move the way your instincts say it should.

To learn to handle your rig, first find a large, empty parking lot or field. Then take your rig, and a trailer-competent friend, over there. When you arrive, start by driving straight ahead, and making various turns. Note the room you need to go around corners. Get the feel of the rig at various speeds and in the turns. Use your **outside mirrors** to see what your trailer is doing as you drive around. After a very little while, you should begin to feel quite confident.

Next, try backing your rig. Try straight backing at first. Keep practicing straight backing until you can move that rig straight as an arrow for as long as you want. This may take a little while as you get used to making the small, but essential, moves on the steering wheel. Strive for smoothness at all times.

TIP

To learn to back up your rig, start the engine and center the front wheels of your tow vehicle. Put one hand at the 6 o'clock position on the steering wheel. To maneuver the trailer, start the tow vehicle slowly moving backwards, and move that hand on the steering in the direction you want the rear *of your trailer to go.*

After you feel that you have mastered straight backing, set up a make-believe, two-lane boat launch ramp. Put something on the ground to simulate the various corners of your ramp. Anything will do for this as long as you can't damage it when you hit it. Traffic cones are ideal, and many times can be borrowed from a road contractor working in the area.

Try backing the rig into your two-lane practice ramp. Back into it from several approach angles until you have a reasonably good feel for how your rig reacts. Just try to stay anywhere on the ramp. You will find that a left approach may seem easier, as you can see better.

Figure 15. *Cuddycabin Launching.* Here is a cuddycabin being launched. Note the close quarters around this ramp, which emphasizes the importance of being in complete control of your boat to avoid collisions.

After you feel reasonably comfortable using the double lane, try using just one of the practice lanes. Practice the same moves you made on the double ramp. This time more precision will be required. You will strive to keep your rig in the one lane at all times.

With this practice, your abilities will soar. It will take, however, several sessions on your practice ramp until you feel really confident. A good instructor will make this learning process easier.

CAUTION!

Never back into an area that you can't completely see. Use a guide, or get out of your tow vehicle and personally check what or who is back there.

After you have practiced to the point where you feel reasonably competent, take your rig out on a quiet road and practice driving in the real world. When you can do this without undue tension, go out to a real launch ramp on a quiet day. Try maneuvering around the ramp's parking lot and backing the trailer down to the water's edge. Do this until you feel comfortable of your abilities around the ramp. It may take several practice visits at that real ramp, but keep practicing until you feel you're ready. If anybody comes to launch or recover while you're there, pull out of the way. Watch to see how they do. You may note that you are now better than they are. Your **first for-real launch** should also be made during a quiet time on the ramp. If you still have trouble backing, don't worry about it. Just keep practicing and it'll come.

Getting Ready to Go

Let's look now at some things you should do as you start out for a boating day. We'll assume that you've just connected your trailer to the tow vehicle.

Figure 16. *Boat Trailer Hooked Up*. Note the safety chains hooked up with the "open" side of the hooks looking to the rear. That's the correct way to keep those chains from jumping out while on the road. The bow stop, winch, jack stand, and spare wheel are visible. Guess he forgot to crank in the winch strap!

Make sure the trailer's coupler is all the way down on the tow vehicle's ball hitch, and that the **coupler latching mechanism** is fully down and locked. Smear a little grease on the ball hitch occasionally to hold down the clanking noises. Shoot WD-40 on the coupler latching mechanism every other trip or so to keep it operating smoothly.

Cross the **safety chains** under the trailer's coupler to their fastening points on the tow vehicle. Your safety chains should be strong enough to support 150 percent of the total weight of your loaded trailer. They should be long enough so you can fully jackknife the rig, but short enough so they don't drag.

Crank the trailer's **jack stand** up and out of the way. Give the jack mechanism some WD-40 when you shoot the coupler latch.

Check the trailer's tire pressures. Normally on single axle trailers, it is maintained at 35 pounds. If there is any doubt about what pressure you need, examine the trailer's Capacity Plate. Don't forget to check the trailer's spare tire.

Connect the trailer's **wiring harness** to the tow vehicle's electrical system. Make sure that *all* the trailer's lights are working.

The trailer's **winch strap** should be fastened to the boat's bow eye and cranked down securely so that the bow is snugged up solidly against the **bow stop.**

The boat's bow should be firmly held down for the road trip by a line, strap, or chain from the bow eye to an eye bolt, or other secure fitting, on the trailer frame.

This bow tie down on the trailer is not provided by some boat dealerships on new trailers, unless you request it. You should.

Next secure the aft end of the boat to the trailer. A common method is by a nylon strap over the gunwales about one-quarter of the way forward from the stern. The ends of this strap are secured to each side of the trailer's main frame and tightly drawn down.

Another good method is to use straps from the two **water-ski towing eyes** on each side of the transom down to fastening points on the trailer's rear frame member.

The method you choose is essentially up to you. We've used both with good results. Our current preference is using the straps from the water ski towing eyes.

Check inside the boat. Everything that can blow away should be secured. All canvas should be tied down to avoid flapping. The heavier things you carry in the boat should be loaded about evenly from front to rear to spread their weight around. Portable fuel tanks should be strapped down securely.

Keep valuable gear in your tow vehicle until ready to launch. This includes VHF radios, GPS units, RADAR units, fish finders and the like. Anything small and expensive is vulnerable.

Place your boat's engine in the manufacturer's recommended **travel position,** securing the lower unit if so recommended.

Lastly, check the **outside mirrors** on your tow vehicle to make sure you can see well behind the tow vehicle. Do this now to avoid fiddling with them while you're rolling.

On the Road

Although operating a trailer boat rig is essentially easy, it is different than simply driving a car.

Cross winds come from Mother Nature and large vehicles traveling at high speeds. They can cause dangerous swaying. If they hit you, slow down by easing off the gas until you feel you have positive control.

Beware of hard braking at any time while underway. Instead, down shift and use your brakes sparingly to maintain control.

Avoid sudden stops and starts with your rig. This is particularly important in turns. A sudden brake application in a turn, for example, almost guarantees a jackknifing skid.

Shift to lower gears for hill climbing and descending. Use your engine rather than brakes on long downhill runs.

Listen for any unusual sounds. An intermittent high-pitched squeal from the trailer, for example, could be a warning of wheel bearing failure.

Take it easy on the road. Visibility to the rear is usually impaired by the boat. Your overall "vehicle" size is usually more than doubled with that boat trailer. More time is required for everything.

Your turns must be wider. Avoid cutting corners and climbing curbs and taking out the stop signs.

Think about the other guy. When you pull out to pass a slow mover, give him plenty of room. If you cut back in too soon you'll sideswipe him.

If any part of your boat is higher than your tow vehicle, be constantly aware of what you are driving under. Things on your boat such as a T-top, anchor lights, and radio antennas can be easily forgotten when you pull off for a rest stop. What you won't soon forget are the wires you tear out, the signs you smash, or the bills you incur.

Check how things are riding after you're down the road about 15 miles. On longer trips we recommend that you pull checks like the following every time you stop. Pull into a safe turn-off and take a few minutes for a walk-around of your rig.

⚓ Look in the boat. Is anything loose? Are all lines secured? Is any canvas flapping? Any spilled liquids? Is the anchor secured? Are all switches off? All tie downs snug?

⚓ Check the trailer's tires. Are they properly inflated? Are all the lug nuts tight? Do the wheels feel tight on the axle?

⚓ Feel the wheel bearings. They should feel warm. If there's a **hot bearing,** you've got a problem to take care of before you go further. If you don't know about making this repair, call for assistance. Driving with a hot trailer wheel bearing is asking for an unpleasant breakdown in the *very* near future.

⚓ Check for any grease being thrown on both sides of each wheel. Loss of grease from the hub may signal a problem, usually a ruptured seal. Whatever caused the leakage should be identified and repaired as soon as possible.

⚓ Check the trailer's coupler. Is it still completely down over the tow ball? Is the latch mechanism down and locked? Is the wiring connector secure? Are the safety chains still hooked up correctly?

The few minutes you take to check your rig are more than repaid if you find and correct something that could ruin your day. From long experience, we can assure you that a breakdown with a loaded trailer boat rig on the highway is something to be avoided if at all possible.

Launching

Let's say now that you've arrived at your destination in good shape and it's time to get ready to launch. Note that you should spend as little time as possible on the launch ramp. This means getting all the preparations taken care of *before* you get on the ramp. Then when it's your turn, you can immediately back your rig down the ramp, get the boat into the water, and clear the ramp with no fiddling around.

Allow your trailer's wheel bearings about 15 minutes to cool off from your road trip before submerging them on the launch. This is about what it takes to get things ready to launch anyway, so that should be no problem. If you dunk warm wheel bearings in colder water, a partial vacuum occurs inside the bearing housing, which can suck in water. This water can do corrosion damage to the bearings.

If you had a **travel cover** on the boat, take it off and secure it in your tow vehicle.

Check your boat over carefully to make sure there was no major damage done while you were on the road. You may not want to launch right then if your boat took a bad flying rock hit that smashed something. If all is OK...

Remove the **boat's tie downs** and stow them in the tow vehicle. Slack off on the winch line a little, but keep it attached to the bow eye.

Prepare your boat's **engine** for use. Remove any travel supports. Tilt the engine to where it will easily clear the ramp as you back down. Check fuel and oil to see if you need immediate servicing. If your boat is equipped with a blower, start it about 15 minutes before launching.

Get the cockpit ready. Install the electronic gear you want to use. Stow the gear you had in the tow vehicle aboard the boat. Untie any items you tied down for the road trip.

Put the **drain plug(s)** in. Double check them.

Unhook the trailer's electrical connector from the tow vehicle. The purpose is of this to make the taillight inoperative, and keep its temperature down. This avoids the sucking of cold water into a hot stop-light fixture, which could blow a fuse and cause damage to the guts of the light. Your stop lights get hot because you're on the brakes a lot when you back down some of the longer ramps.

Walk down and quickly eyeball the launch ramp. Look for any objects on the ramp that might injure your tires, pick them up, and put them in the trash. Look into the water at the end of the ramp and on both sides for any obstructions or dropoffs. Notice the prevailing winds and if there are any currents around the ramp that would affect your boat when launching. Now walk back up to your boat and...

Attach the bow line to the bow eye or bow cleat. If it is windy, or there is a strong current, attach another line to a stern cleat. This is so the boat can be completely controlled from the shore after it floats off the trailer.

While you're doing all this, keep an eye on the launch ramp for any problem other boaters may be having. One of the most common is loss of traction on the ramp due to water draining off recovering boats. This may be no real problem when you're launching, but you want to be aware of ramp conditions as much as possible.

When it's your turn, back the rig straight down to the water's edge, aligning the trailer at right angles to the water's edge. *Stop, get out, and check the drain plug(s) again.* We'll spare you the horror stories about launching with the drain plugs out, but you can imagine what happens if you forget them.

Ideally you should have one person in the boat and another at the water's edge to help guide the tow vehicle operator. If you don't, there's no real problem. It just takes a little longer to get the boat launched.

With a standard bunk trailer, back it into the water until the boat just floats free. If you have a tilt bed or roller trailer, you need not back into the water nearly as far. Usually the boat will move off the tilt bed or roller trailer with very little effort when the winch hook is released.

With the boat floating free, put your tow vehicle's transmission in Park and the parking brakes On. Get out and place **chocks** behind each rear wheel of your tow vehicle. Scrap 4×4s are good for this.

Lower the boat's engine or outdrive and start the engine. After it fires up, check for normal operation of the engine's cooling and other systems. Let it run for a minute or so, and then alternately put it in Reverse and Forward. If it doesn't quit, you're ready to move the boat away from the ramp area. If it does quit, give it about a minute more warm-up, and try it again. If you can't keep the engine running after those tries, you'd better abort the launch until you can get it operating properly.

If you're ready to proceed with the launch, the **winch** cable can now be released from the bow eye, and the boat moved either to a nearby pier, beached, or whatever. The bow and stern lines can be used to help guide the boat after it floats off the trailer, if necessary.

Back at the trailer, crank in and secure the winch cable. Check to make sure you didn't leave anything on the ramp. Then drive the tow vehicle and empty trailer slowly up the launch ramp and park it. Try to locate it where you won't be blocked in by others who launch after you. Lock everything securely.

To make your **recovery** easier, put some liquid detergent on the trailer's boat support carpeting. Then when you submerge the trailer to receive your boat, the bunks will be really slick.

Recovery

If you are using a busy facility, there will probably be a line of boats waiting to recover. Before you join that happy herd, drop off the tow vehicle operator on shore so that your trailer will be ready when your turn comes to use the ramp. As you get in the line of boats, the tow vehicle operator now goes to the parking lot, gets the trailer ready, and joins the line at the top of the ramp. Then when it's time, the trailer is backed down the ramp and into the water to the proper depth to receive the boat.

The proper depth depends on the trailer you have. You should experiment with what works best for your rig. After some fooling around (read "experimenting"), we learned to submerge our present trailer to the first amber running light on its frame. This works fine on the launch ramps on *our* waterways. You must find out what's best for *your* situation.

If you have a drive-on trailer, drive the boat on to the trailer, or winch her up. How you do this depends on your boat size and type, the trailer you have, and the wind and water conditions.

There's a knack to this that is best learned by practicing with your individual boat and trailer on a quiet ramp. We have found that it's best if you approach a drive-on trailer at a slow pace, maintaining full **steerageway.** Maneuver your boat so it is centered and square with the back of the trailer as you hit it. Then, when the boat is solidly on the trailer, increase your engine RPM, go hands-off on the wheel, and let the bunks take her all the way home hard against the bow stop. Then chop the throttle.

If you don't have a drive-on trailer, move the boat up the trailer with its engine as far as possible, and then pull her up all the way to the bow stop by hand and winch.

If your boat is not resting properly on the trailer after all this, back it off and reload. If you pull an improperly-loaded boat out of the water, and then later attempt to adjust its position on the trailer while on land, you'll be making a difficult job for yourself. To avoid major **hull damage,** it is important for your boat to be positioned properly on its trailer before any travel.

With the boat properly on the trailer, secure it as follows:

First, hook the winch line to the bow eye and draw it down tight. Snub that bow solidly against the bow chock.

Next raise your engine, or the outdrive, so it won't drag on the ramp.

Now drive the rig partway up the ramp. Stop and pull the drain plug(s) to clear the bilge. Then move on up the ramp to make it available for the next user. With the rig in a parking area, get things ready for the next road trip.

Slick Ramp Tricks

In your trailer boating adventures, you will find that many times the launch ramp is slick from water, weeds, algae, ice, and whatever. This causes major problems to many folks as they try to recover their boats.

The first reaction of many trailer boaters when faced with lack of ramp traction is to gun the tow vehicle engine, and hope the tires grab. You see this usually futile action all the time during slick conditions. What happens is a lot of tire howling and smoking, with a sideways drift of the rig toward the weeds. It's not a pretty sight.

We can help you, however, with these time-proven slick ramp techniques.

Spread some sand out to about five feet ahead of the tow vehicle's drive wheel. We keep a bucket of sand in the tow vehicle for these occasions.

Deflate the drive wheel's tire to where the sidewall deflects enough to increase traction. *You must re-air that tire before you go on the highway, or you'll ruin the tire.*

Stick one of those mud and snow gripper strips you can buy in auto parts stores, under the drive wheel.

Get out your tow strap and ask for towing help on top of the ramp. A vehicle pulling from up there where it is usually not slick can get your rig moving quite easily. It's helpful to keep about 75 feet of nylon tow strap in your tow vehicle for this, and other, such purposes.

If you have a **front bumper hitch,** disconnect the trailer, swap tow vehicle ends, and drag the trailer out.

If you have a **front-end mounted winch** on your tow vehicle, hook the winch cable to something solid on top of the ramp, and drag your entire rig up the ramp.

One, or several of these tips used together, will put you and your rig up the ramp and back on top.

Random Trailering Thoughts

All ramp problems seem to get worse in direct proportion to the number of folks waiting to launch and recover. Do your part by learning to recover promptly and clearing the ramp area with minimum delay.

Many folks really worry about getting their boat in and out of the water without:

⚓ Looking too stupid

⚓ Damaging or hurting something or someone

⚓ Having to get help from somebody, thereby tarnishing their "boating expert" image

⚓ All of the above

A lot of this is vanity in trying to look "professional." Don't worry about it. You've done your part by learning to properly handle your rig, and are, or soon will be, as good or better than most recreational boaters.

Don't get uptight over the very few inconsiderate folks who seem to come out on national holidays and hoot and holler like a bunch of crazies. They'll soon fade away like the fog in the morning, and leave the waterways for real power boaters like you.

NOTES

NOTES

Chapter 4

~~~~~~

Operating the Boat—
You're the Skipper

> *This chapter provides you with important boat operating information as the Skipper.*

As the Skipper you have some very singular obligations. You must always remember that:

> *You are legally and morally responsible for the safety of your vessel and the lives of everyone aboard.*

Think about that. Realize how important it is that you gain asound knowledge of the many things involved in power boating.

Our sport is a lifetime source of tremendous pleasure for those who learn about it in the right way, *and* practice what they learn. Those folks who can't, or won't, grasp what boating really involves, usually give it up soon after the novelty wears off.

IMPORTANT

We strongly recommend that you expand on what we give you here by participating in any formal boating courses offered in your area. In addition to acquiring the really useful information, you will meet some fine folks.

The excellent educational programs and other activities offered by the **United States Coast Guard Auxiliary** in many communities, are designed to satisfy the requirements of most recreational boaters. Ask at any Coast Guard unit, or call 1-800-336-BOAT for complete information.

Each of the 400-plus **U.S. Power Squadrons (USPS)** offer several outstanding educational programs. The annual USPS Boating Course is open to the general public, while other programs are for members only. These member courses include seamanship, pilotage, navigation, engine maintenance, electronics, and weather topics. Call 1-800-828-3380 for additional information.

The **American Red Cross** has a variety of life-saving courses and material on boating safety. Check your telephone directory for a local number.

There are also courses and seminars available through boat dealerships and sporting goods stores, or in some locales, through adult education programs. Your boat dealer, or local newspaper's outdoor editor, should be able to give you information on these programs.

Safety Afloat

The **United States Coast Guard** has analyzed the data from a large number of **fatal boating accident** reports over recent years. These data show that two-thirds of all fatal boating accidents are caused by falls overboard and capsizing. These accidents are usually the results of overloading the boat, improper weight distribution, high speed maneuvers, leaning over the side, and operator inattention or carelessness. The other one-third of fatal boating accidents are caused by sinking, swamping/flooding, collision, and "other." Coast Guard studies indicate that **alcohol** consumption is involved in more than half of all boating accidents. Think about it. Over 50 percent of all boating accidents could be avoided if bottle and throttle were not mixed.

The Coast Guard has the authority to enforce the Federal boating laws on all Federal waters. Each state boating agency has enforcement authority on its state waters for *both* Federal and state boating laws.

Federal, and most state enforcement authorities, will take action if a boat is observed being operated in an **"unsafe condition,"** as defined by law or regulation.

If it is determined that an **"especially hazardous condition"** exists, the boat Skipper will be required to take immediate steps to correct the condition, including returning to port. **Mandatory voyage termination** by the authorities may be imposed for any one of the following:

⚓ Insufficient number of approved Personal Floatation Devices (PFDs)

⚓ Insufficient fire extinguishers

⚓ Overloading beyond the boat manufacturer's recommended safe-loading capacity

⚓ Improper navigation light display

⚓ Non-compliance with the ventilation requirements for fuel tank and engine

⚓ Fuel leakage

⚓ Fuel in bilges

⚓ Improper backfire flame control

⚓ Operating in regulated boating areas during predetermined adverse conditions (13th Coast Guard District only)

⚓ Manifestly unsafe voyage

It is contrary to Federal law to operate a vessel in a "negligent" or "grossly negligent" manner. Some examples of **"negligent operations"** or **"grossly negligent**

operations" are as follows (the nature and circumstances of the violation determines which is which):

⚓ Operating a boat in a swimming area

⚓ Operating a boat while under the influence of alcohol or drugs

⚓ Excessive speed in the vicinity of other boats or in dangerous waters

⚓ Hazardous water skiing practices

Many states have established **speed limits,** and other operating restrictions, in and around certain events and locations. These include regattas and races, as well as public beaches. A check should be made with your State Boating Office regarding any such restrictions.

The Coast Guard has conducted tests to see how the **fatigue** caused by a normal marine environment affects the boat's Skipper. Factors included typical wave and water motion, vibration, engine noise, sun, wind, and spray. It was discovered that, under normal conditions, with no alcohol of any kind, the Skipper suffers serious fatigue impairment in coordination and reaction time after only a few hours. If alcohol is involved, this normal fatigue compounds the effect of the alcohol, and sharply increases the accident potential.

IMPORTANT

The marine environment is unforgiving. What starts out as a minor problem can rapidly escalate into a major crisis. You must be in full control of your faculties at all times in order to avoid disastrous consequences.

Operating a boat while under the influence of alcohol, or any other drug, is dangerous to you, your passengers, and others on the water. This is a proven point, no matter how good you feel, how supremely confident you are, or what the "good life" beer ads show on TV. Tragic drownings, and other fatal accidents, happen all too frequently to those who choose to disregard this fact.

As a result of the dangers involved, and the persistent ignoring of the hazards involved in on-the-water substance abuse, the Coast Guard has developed a three-fold plan to reduce these drug-related accidents. This consists of increased and widespread education to develop public awareness, enhanced law enforcement, and an improved **accident reporting system.**

Accidents

As the Skipper, you are required by law to report certain accidents to local authorities.

When to Report:

⚓ If there is damage by, or to, a vessel or its equipment that exceeds $500, or there is complete loss of the vessel. Note that many states have set limits less than $500. Check with local authorities for the amount in your area

⚓ If there is injury or loss of life

⚓ If there is disappearance of any person on board a vessel under circumstances indicating death or injury

What to Report:

⚓ **Boating accidents** include collision, capsizing, sinking, grounding, falls overboard, strikes by boat or propeller, swamping, flooding, fire, explosion, disappearance (other than theft).

Time Limits to Report:

⚓ 48 hours if there is loss of life

⚓ 48 hours if there is injury requiring medical treatment beyond first aid

⚓ 48 hours in case of disappearance of a person from a vessel

⚓ 10 days if there is only damage to the vessel and/or property

How to Report:

⚓ The Coast Guard **Boating Accident Report Form** may be used in all cases of accident reporting. Copies of the Boating Accident Report Form, information on state dollar-damage reporting thresholds, and other valuable boating safety information is available through your State Boating Office.

Who Must Report:

⚓ The Boating Accident Report Form is usually filled out by the Skipper, unless he is physically unable to complete the form. In that case, the owner of the vessel must submit the form.

Why Report?

⚓ A report must be filed because the information supplied is used to develop safety regulations and manufacturing standards for the benefit of the boating public. The information is also used in boating safety education programs and other boating safety initiatives. Without good data, a boating safety hazard might be completely overlooked, and other boaters could be hurt.

If you need additional assistance in reporting an accident, call the **Coast Guard Boating Safety Hotline** at **1-800-368-5647.** If you are in the Washington, D.C. area the local number is 267-0780. Hotline operators are on duty Monday through Friday from 8:00 a.m. to 4:00 p.m., Eastern Time. At other times, an answering machine will take your name and telephone number and an operator will call you back the next working day.

Another important part of the Hotline service is the identification of safety problems in recreational boats.

When you report a safety problem, the information you provide is carefully evaluated. If it is determined that the problem represents a safety defect in some product, its manufacturer will be asked to conduct a **safety recall.**

This requires the manufacturer to send a written notice to all registered owners informing them of the defect. As it is difficult for a manufacturer to keep track of every owner, it may not be possible to send the mail notice to everyone who owns the boat or engine named in the recall.

So if you are buying a used boat or engine, and are wondering if either item has ever been involved in a safety recall, call the Hotline and find out. If your items have been so involved, the Hotline operator will inform you how to get the manufacturer to correct the problem.

If you prefer to write for further Hotline information, address your request to:

Consumer Affairs Staff (G-BC)
Office of Consumer Affairs
U.S. Coast Guard Headquarters
Washington, DC 20593-0001

Emergencies

The good Skipper should plan for situations that are potentially the most life-threatening. Here are four dangerous situations:

Fire on the Boat

If you maintain a high standard of cleanliness and maintenance, your chances of a fire aboard are greatly reduced. Despite all precautions, however, fires do occur on vessels while underway. Their danger cannot be over-emphasized. Your habitat afloat, indeed your life, is gravely threatened. You must have a practiced **fire plan** for this most serious threat to your vessel.

Here are some suggestions. Note that these are not necessarily in the order to be taken. That order depends entirely on the circumstances.

⚓ Direct all persons aboard to put on their Personal Floatation Device (PFD) immediately.

⚓ Turn the boat to keep the fire blowing downwind and away from the more flammable areas on the boat. Reduce headway to dead stop.

⚓ If the fire is in an engine, shut that engine down; turn all electrical circuits off; turn off main fuel valve.

⚓ If practical, throw burning items over the side. Close all windows, hatches, and port holes to better confine the fire.

⚓ Move any portable fuel tanks, and other containers of flammable materials, as far away from the fire as possible.

⚓ Use water to extinguish paper, cloth and wood blazes; use your fire extinguishers on all other fires.

⚓ Call for assistance by radio, or by other means, as required.

Person Overboard

The level of danger to a person falling overboard ranks all the way from nil to death. It all depends on the circumstances and the way you, as Skipper, react. If the overboard occurs in the daytime, in warm water, pleasant weather, with little boat traffic, and the person is uninjured, has on his PFD, can swim well, and there are no sharks around, then the danger level may be nil, and it all could be great fun.

A fall overboard in less benign circumstances, however, requires swift, positive, practiced responses. We strongly recommend that each Skipper develop a recovery procedure for his vessel, and practice it on a regular basis.

Here are some techniques to consider in getting the person overboard back in your boat:

Reduce your headway as promptly as possible. Turn back to where the person is in the water. Your plan should include instructions for a designated person on board to keep his eye on the person overboard at all times to the maximum extent possible. A person in the water can be quickly lost from sight if there are any waves, or if visibility is in any way restricted. Throwing something large and brightly colored into the water as close as possible to the overboard person can be very helpful.

Also, if a person falls overboard at night, or in high wave conditions, immediately throw overboard any form of floating debris, such as torn-up newspapers or magazine pages, or anything else that may be readily spotted on the water. This may help you return to about the same spot where the incident occurred. This is important as a person in the water can be extremely hard to locate under poor light or wave conditions.

If your boat is equipped with a Global Positioning System (GPS), your boat's present position can be remembered by the device. Certain models have a feature for entering the location to be remembered by a single keystroke. This would be very useful in locating a person overboard.

When you locate the person in the water, it is usually best to maneuver your boat around to approach from downwind. When you are close, throw a line with some floating object such as a life jacket tied on the end. Once the overboard person has the line in hand, reduce your throttle setting to Neutral or **Dead Slow** if the temporary loss of headway will not endanger the vessel. Once the person seizes the lifeline, carefully pull him back on board.

It is usually best if no one else enters the water to help the victim, unless absolutely essential. If so, that other person should always put on his PFD before entering the water, *and* carry a line attached to the vessel.

Pulling a person out of the water and back on board can be a surprisingly difficult task. This is particularly so if the person overboard is incapacitated in any way, is of large stature, darkness has fallen, the weather is foul, the water is cold, or your boat has a high freeboard.

Remember, there is particular danger at night, in adverse weather, high waves, cold water, and where a child, elderly person, injured or incapacitated person is involved.

IMPORTANT

The recovery of an overboard person must be practiced regularly, particularly if you operate on big water, or where the hazard level, for whatever reason, is high.

Collision

As used here, **"collision"** means boats striking each other, or a boat striking a man-made or natural object. As the number of boats on our waterways increase, so does the probability of collision. This is due, of course, to the congestion created by the additional boats, as well as by the increased number of inexperienced Skippers.

The best way to avoid a collision is to keep a sharp lookout at all times, obey the marine "Rules of the Road," and yield the right-of-way as the situation warrants.

On many of our waterways, certain folks don't keep a sharp lookout or obey the "Rules of the Road," and always insist on the right-of-way. Sadly, the same jerks you dodge on the highway are also out there on the water, behaving the same way with their boats. So facing those unpleasant facts, here are a few ideas on handling the **aftermath of a collision:**

Immediately stop your boat away from other boat traffic, if possible. Turn your bilge pumps on. All persons aboard should immediately put on their PFDs.

Determine if there are any injuries among the people involved. Necessary first aid should be performed. Help should be immediately sought as required. If there is danger of sinking, or there are serious personal injuries, outside assistance should be immediately requested.

The boat(s) involved should be inspected by their Skippers without delay to determine if there is any below-the-waterline hull damage. Bilge pumps should be run until the hull damages are determined and emergency repairs completed as needed. If a hull is ruptured below the waterline, the hole(s) must be found and plugged with whatever materials are available to slow or stop the water flow.

If the bilge pumps aren't enough, then start bailing, using whatever containers are available. The essential thing is to get as much water out of the boat as possible.

Big water boats are well advised to carry **hull-rupture plugs** available from many boat supply houses. These conically-shaped plugs can be jammed into holes in the hull, and they will significantly slow down the water flow.

Collisions with underwater obstacles are very common, particularly among fishermen. The extent of damage done is usually related to the speed being traveled and the nature of the underwater object struck. The most common damage is to the lower unit of the engine, and/or to the propeller. Hull damage usually occurs if contact is made with hard underwater objects at cruise speed. These collisions are usually not life-menacing as such, but they can be a major hassle. It can get awfully expensive if you charge around in a big hurry where the water gets skinny, and there are things in that water that can clobber you.

Propeller Trouble

Propeller problems are a common predicament for many boaters. If you're like most of us, your propeller will hit underwater obstructions from time to time. If you spend all your time dragging water skiers around the lake, this will probably not be too frequent. But if you like to fish, and poke around looking for Old Lunker, you'll be hitting things every time you launch.

To prevent serious damage to boat engines and lower units, almost every manufacturer has designed either a

shear pin or **slip clutch** into their engine's power train.

Shear pins are utilized on smaller outboard engines, usually under 40 HP. The pin breaks when that propeller takes a hit from an underwater obstruction. When this happens, the propeller spins freely, the engine overspeeds, but major damage to the engine is usually prevented. You, however, need to put in a new shear pin to get going again.

This involves removing the propeller, clearing out the pieces of the broken shear pin, and installing the new one. If you haven't actually done this before, it's a good idea to change out a shear pin for the practice.

Get out your Engine Owner's Handbook to check how it should be done on your particular engine. You'll need a couple of things for this job. These include needle-nose pliers, a wrench that fits your propeller's retaining nut, the new shear pin, a new cotter pin, and some marine grease to put on the **drive shaft splines.**

If you replace the shear pin over water, you will discover how easy it is to drop stuff while working. Have several extra shear pins available, and hang on to your tools tightly. We recommend you try this first in shallow water over a hard sand bottom, or else in your driveway.

On larger engines, the slip clutch is standard. This consists of a propeller with an inner rubber hub which grips the propeller shaft. It is tightly fitted so that under normal use there is no slippage. If the propeller takes a solid hit, the rubber hub slips, preventing any real damage to the engine. No subsequent repair action is required in most such cases.

Occasionally some **"retained slippage"** will occur on a slip clutch propeller after it strikes an obstruction. This is usually not a serious problem. You can get home by running at a reduced RPM to keep the propeller from slipping. Get this propeller repaired as soon as possible.

Even though most propellers are extremely reliable and complete failures are not too common, we recommend that all boaters carry a spare propeller. Experience has shown that when you need that spare you need it real bad. It is cheap **get-home insurance.**

Getting Help

The key element in getting assistance is making your request for help in the right way. That sounds obvious, but, in the turmoil of an emergency, good sense tends to be back on the dock, unless you are well trained and practiced in what must be done.

"Distress," as used here, is where your boat is threatened by grave, imminent danger, requiring immediate assistance.

Here are some forms of distress signals from the **International and Inland Rules of the Road:**

Red meteor flares	Red parachute flares
Smoke	Flames in a bucket
Code flags	Dye marker in water
Fog horn	Gun fired once per minute
Radio calls	Waving arms or flag
Position beacon	High intensity strobe

In coastal waters, an orange flag waved from side to side is a recognized emergency signal. The inverted United States flag is another distress signal.

In areas where the Coast Guard provides **Search and Rescue (SAR)** service, and in many other areas where there is significant boating traffic, the Very High Frequency (VHF) and Single Side Band (SSB) radios are the primary communications tools.

The Citizens Band (CB) radio is used by some boaters, sometimes alone, and sometimes in combination with the

VHF. The CB, however, is not monitored by most Coast Guard stations, and you may wind up chatting with some Good Buddy in an 18-wheeler on the Interstate.

The cellular telephone is coming into increased use on inland and coastal waters as service is expanded and quality improved. If you plan to use this means, find out the telephone numbers you need to get assistance while afloat.

If you are in distress, the following radio procedures should be used. This same information can also be provided over a cellular phone. Speak slowly and clearly:

"MAYDAY...MAYDAY...MAYDAY"

"This is (say your boat's name)" Repeat three times.

"MAYDAY (say your boat's name again).

Give your location.

State the nature of your distress.

Give the number and condition of the persons aboard your boat.

State the seaworthiness of your boat.

Give your boat's length, type, color, and anything else that will help rescuers find you.

"I will be listening on (Channel 16 VHF)."

"This is (name of boat), over"

Someone should answer if within your VHF range (around 20 miles). If not, keep trying.

The Coast Guard will take immediate steps to help you once they hear your MAYDAY. Normally, the Coast Guard, or Coast Guard Auxiliary rescue boats, and/or aircraft will be sent. However, assistance from other sources may be arranged to speed your rescue.

When you are not in real distress, but still need help, the Coast Guard may be contacted as above. Substitute the expression PAN PAN (pronounced PAWN PAWN) for MAY-DAY. If you want to report a navigational hazard encountered, use the expression SECURITY (pronounced SAY-CUR-I-TAY) in place of the MAYDAY.

MAYDAY is from the French *m'aidez* (help me). It originated during World War I where it was used by Allied aviators. PAN PAN is the English version of the French word *panne,* the maritime use of which means helpless, breakdown, no power, etc. SECURITY is the international French appellation for "safety."

The **Coast Guard's Search and Rescue (SAR)** role is to assist mariners in distress. If you are not in life-threatening distress, and alternative sources of assistance are available, the Coast Guard will normally coordinate efforts to assist you.

If you have a friend, marina, or commercial firm you want contacted, the Coast Guard will attempt to do so. If this is not successful, the Coast Guard will make a **Marine Request Assistance Broadcast (MARB)** on VHF Channel 16. This announces that you need help, gives your location, and invites others to your aid.

A **commercial towing firm** may offer its services. *Be aware that if you accept this help you will have to pay for these services.*

Understand that there is the possibility of damage to your boat during towing and salvage operations. Your help provider should have the proper insurance to protect you and your boat if they cause damage. You should also make sure that the operator has a valid Coast Guard license.

It is important to agree on a price with the commercial firm before any service is provided. Clearly understand the exact type of assistance being offered, and how much it's going to cost, before accepting any help from a potential provider.

You may also receive offers of help from non-commercial sources. These could include fellow mariners in the area, or some local public agency. Keep in mind that these **Good Samaritans,** although certainly well-meaning, may not have the equipment or skills needed to safely and effectively help you. Further damage to your boat and passengers could occur due to their actions. This could result in serious difficulties if you later seek restitution through the courts.

After you have contacted the Coast Guard for assistance, keep in contact with them at regular intervals before and after help arrives. They also should be advised if your conditions change sufficiently to cause alarm and/or require SAR action.

It is important that you *never abandon your boat* without leaving some sort of written notification about your intentions. Even then, salvage operators may take possession of your abandoned boat. It is far preferable to leave someone on board, or very nearby if beached, if at all possible.

Helping Others

It is a long-standing tradition among sailors to help each other. Here are a few thoughts about this important topic.

While it is clearly your moral responsibility to help others if any *lives* are in jeopardy, we do not believe that you have any moral responsibility if only property is involved. You must make a careful appraisal of the situation and be a Good Samaritan *only* if you can provide the assistance without unduly risking your boat or passengers.

There are times when the best help you can give is to stand off nearby, make sure help has been summoned, and await the arrival of more qualified assistance.

One of the most common ways of helping a fellow mariner in distress is to provide a tow back to shore. This procedure is useful to learn. Towing another boat, however, can present certain hazards, so do not attempt even the most simple tows until you know the basic principles. Tow lines can break under tension and snap back with tremendous force. Arms and legs can be crushed or broken if caught between close-by, heaving boats.

Find a qualified person, or training program, to teach you these techniques. Here are a few thoughts to give you an overview of the process:

If a relatively small boat is to be towed, and the weather and seas are favorable, a water-ski towing bridle is an effective means of fastening the tow line to your boat.

If a larger boat is involved, a bridle similar to the water-ski bridle, but of heavier line, can be easily constructed. The bridle is secured to the water ski tow eyes, or stern cleats, of your boat. Braided nylon is effective as a tow line. One-half inch diameter should be more than adequate for most protected inland waters.

Once everything is rigged on your tow boat, the tow line must be gotten to the boat being towed. If the weather is good, and the sea conditions permit, move your boat into throwing range. It is usually best to approach the disabled boat from the downwind side. The line can then be heaved across the bow of the disabled boat.

If conditions are such that you can't safely heave the tow line, position your boat upwind of the disabled boat. **Bend** (means "tie," when you're afloat) a buoyant cushion, or other PFD, to the tow line and float it over.

The tow line should be fastened to the **bow eye,** or **bow cleat,** on the centerline of the boat being towed. The line is fastened to the towing boat at the connecting **bight** (loop) in the towing bridle.

Once the tow line has been made fast to the disabled boat, and her Skipper has signaled an OK to you, slowly take up the slack between the two boats and increase to a suitable towing speed. The towing speed is dependent on weather and sea conditions, the type of vessels involved, and the skill of the Skippers. At the least, you should maintain adequate headway in the towing vessel so that you have positive steering control.

Now see how the towed boat is riding. Adjust your speed so that she rides straight behind you without **yawing** (swinging back and forth off the course line), or showing other signs of instability.

Depending on the sea conditions, you may have to adjust the length of the tow line while underway to avoid unnecessary surging between the boats.

As you leave the open water and approach the shoreside destination, reduce speed, and shorten the tow line as necessary. Swing wide around buoys, and other obstructions, so the towed boat has ample room to clear.

Terminating the tow should be done at **no-wake** (very slow) speed. It usually is best to attempt to keep your towing boat clear of the dock or shore and allow the towed boat to drift in to the desired spot. The Skipper of the towed boat should release the tow line at the last minute. You should then pull well away and recover your tow line, being careful to avoid your propeller(s).

Remember, certain tow jobs may be beyond your capabilities. Rather than attempting a dangerous tow, your best action may be to call qualified help. Then stand off at a safe distance ready to assist in case there is an on-board emergency, until that help arrives.

Helmsmanship

One of the things that will mark you as a good **helmsman** is your ability to "stay ahead of the boat." This means anticipating events in order to take advance action to avoid problems. We believe that alertness is a key attribute. Being sensitive to all that's going on is essential. You must be *constantly* aware of what's happening on, and around, your vessel. The Coast Guard estimates that lack of alertness due to intoxication, fatigue, and stress is responsible for over 50 percent of all boating accidents.

Steering

Following are some thoughts to help you better understand just what's happening when the various engine and steering controls are activated:

The engine's propeller forces water through itself as it turns under power. The ejected water forms a column due to the way the propeller's blades are shaped and positioned on its hub. The effect of this moving column of water on the surrounding water is called "thrust."

If that thrust is exactly parallel with the boat's **centerline,** the boat will move straight ahead. If the thrust is at an angle to the centerline, the boat will turn. The size of the angle between the boat's centerline and the propeller's line of thrust, and the amount of that thrust, determine the rapidity and sharpness of the resulting turn.

In the **Inboard engine** the propeller, and its line of thrust, are permanently fixed parallel to the boat's centerline. The propeller's thrust column is deflected by a rudder, as controlled from the helm, which causes the turning effect. In the **Outboard,** and the **Inboard/Outboard,** the propeller and its thrust column move directly with the movement of the tiller or the steering wheel.

The amount of thrust is controlled by your engine's throttle. As you open the throttle, the engine's RPM and thrust increase. Close the throttle and the RPM and thrust decrease.

One of the keys to superior helmsmanship is becoming completely familiar with your boat's response to various throttle settings and steering wheel or tiller positions. This is best learned through actual experience on the water with your vessel.

It's important to know where your propeller is "looking" at all times. As you can't actually see the propeller while at the helm, it's useful to have a reference on the steering wheel itself. Some boats come equipped with a pointer attached to the moving steering wheel shaft, and a fixed card mounted on the shaft housing. If the pointer is centered on the card, the propeller is looking down the boat's centerline. Advancing the throttle will then send the boat off in a straight line.

If you don't have such an arrangement on your boat, and you think it would be handy, put a reference mark on the steering wheel like this:

⚓ Before you start your engine, center your steering wheel so the propeller is looking to the rear, straight down the boat's centerline. Wrap a width of colored plastic tape at the very top of the steering wheel.

⚓ By checking the position of that tape whenever you apply power, you will be sure where your propeller is looking, and of the resulting direction of the engine's thrust.

You can't steer a power boat when the engine is shut down and the propeller is not turning. Don't laugh. It's tried all the time. Just look around some nice Sunday

Figure 17. Robalo 2650 Cuddycabin Underway. Note the twin outboards on this 26-footer. Most two-engine boats are set up with counter-rotating propellers. *Photograph courtesy of US Marine.*

afternoon at any marina and see all those steering wheels being turned and the stopped props waving around as folks lurch in.

Remember, there are no brakes on your power boat! You stop the boat by reversing the direction your propeller is rotating, and then applying enough power to halt the boat's movement. You can also cut the power, and drift to a stop in some situations.

Trimming

A boat's "trim" determines the way she rides the water both at rest and while underway. The trim is achieved by how you load your boat, *and* by the way the engine's thrust is directed while underway.

Loading your boat by spreading the weight around and keeping it low in the vessel is important. Care should be taken to keep your total load under the specified weight limitation for that hull. See the Coast Guard plate on your vessel for this information.

After your boat is loaded properly, the other aspect of trimming involves controlling the boat's bow angle while underway. This is accomplished by changing the angle of the engine's thrust with respect to the boat's horizontal axis.

You should know that in a boat equipped with a single engine mounted on the stern:

A "bow-up" condition can be achieved by directing the engine's thrust downward from the horizontal; and,

A "bow-down" condition comes from directing that thrust upwards.

Adjusting the angle of thrust is usually accomplished in the larger outboards and stern-drive units by a built-in **trim control.** In addition, some boats are equipped with **trim tabs** which can be either fixed, or controlled from the helm. In the smaller outboards, the trim angle is fixed. It is manually adjusted when the engine is not running.

You will normally get the highest speed for your RPM setting, plus the best fuel economy, when your boat is trimmed in a slight bow-up position.

"Bow-up" or "bow-down," as used here, does not necessarily mean all the way up, or down. It refers to the up or down points you determine from your load and the wind and wave conditions. Changes to your boat's trim will be required as these conditions vary.

You will note the effect of your engine's **torque** while underway. As normally set up, this causes your boat to want to turn to the left when you are trimmed to a bow-up position. When you trim bow-down, your boat will want to turn to the right. The path of these torque-induced forces depend upon the rotation direction of the propeller.

You will normally trim slightly bow-down when you want to accelerate your boat onto the plane. Bow-down is also used to pull a load, such as towing another boat, or while dragging water skiers around. You can also use the plowing effect of a slight bow-down trim to ease the porpoising that some boats experience in certain wave and wind conditions. Fuel consumption is increased by this trim position, but that is more than compensated for by a smoother ride.

When your boat is properly trimmed you will realize the maximum speed for the RPM you set, and get the best gas mileage as well. In addition, you will enjoy the most comfortable ride for the existing conditions.

Practice

On-water practice is productive and very enjoyable. Do your practicing both on relatively calm days with few other people around, as well as in windy and congested conditions. Try to experience as many varied situations as possible. Keep a record of what you practice and the weather and sea conditions at the time. As you do this, you will note a sharp rise in your proficiency and confidence.

Try your boat in as many maneuvers, and at various speeds, as possible. Bring her on and off plane, straight ahead and in turns. Really try to get the feel of the boat. Keep her trimmed right so she'll run straight almost "hands-off." Now do the following:

Try the lower RPM straight ahead and in turns, and see how she reacts. You'll probably have to add more power to keep her up on plane as the sharpness of your turns increases.

Determine the boat's minimum turning radius. This is most useful to know when you are moving in restricted areas.

Try backing at varying speeds, both straight and in turns. See how much water comes over the transom.

Try stopping the boat from various Forward and Reverse speeds and see how much distance it takes each time, and how she reacts.

Try all the controls to see the effect of each on the boat while underway. Really get to know how your boat behaves in various wind and current conditions.

Try maneuvering her under varying wind, wave, and current conditions in the open water and in close quarters. Try her with the power off, at Neutral, and at various RPM. It is important that the helmsman be constantly aware of the wind condition, and its velocity, and that he use it to the best possible advantage.

Get to know what **"crab" angle** you must put on your boat's bow to get back onto your trailer in different wind and current conditions. The crab angle is the bow angle off a straight line between where you are and your destination point. You "crab" the boat by turning into a cross wind or current enough to give you the shortest track to your destination.

Strive at all times for smoothness. Jerky steering and erratic throttle movements are a sure sign of inexperience, incompetence, or inattention. If you consciously seek smoothness, it will come much faster than you think possible. Practicing all this will do wonders to improve your abilities. We read somewhere that theory is about 20 percent of the process in becoming a good helmsman, with the other 80 percent learned on the water.

WARNING

Some combinations of wind, waves, throttle, and trim can cause uncontrollable steering forces as you advance the throttle. Therefore, always start at the lower engine RPMs and work up slowly and smoothly. If you notice any heavy control forces, immediately close (reduce) the throttle.

A competent helmsman understands the effects of the various control settings on the boat in the different wind and wave conditions. He knows how to safely avoid *and* recover from hazardous situations.

Heavy Seas

When first noticing adverse conditions, the Skipper must decide whether he wants to seek shelter or keep on course. Seeking shelter can be as simple as hiding out from a passing thunderstorm in a cove on an inland lake, or as complex as a major course change in order to put a large land mass between you and an arriving cold front on big water.

Once you get behind a land mass, it is generally better to seek shelter on its **windward side.** This is the side from which the wind blows. The water there is much calmer. The

lee side is the direction toward which the wind is blowing. Seas to the **leeward** are usually much rougher due to wind-induced wave action.

If the decision is made to proceed into the weather the Skipper should:

- ⚓ Insure that all aboard put on their Personal Flotation Devices
- ⚓ Break out and rig any needed emergency items, to include the bailing gear, sea anchor, throwable life preservers, and extra line
- ⚓ Run the pumps to get the bilge as dry as possible before getting into the weather disturbance
- ⚓ Stow or lash all loose gear, close and **dog (lock)** all hatches and windows
- ⚓ Switch to the fullest fuel tank
- ⚓ Extinguish all open flames
- ⚓ Get a good position fix to know where you were when the adverse weather was encountered.

Your boat's speed is critical in most sea conditions. It is usually best to maintain **steerageway** (positive steering) at all times. The following will help you maintain control:

- ⚓ When heading into **heavy seas,** hold your bow at an angle of about 45 degrees to the line of waves.
- ⚓ You must react immediately with throttle and helm if you are forced off course. Do not allow the boat to wallow. Keep it going on course with enough power.
- ⚓ If you are running downwind before the sea, maintain enough forward speed to avoid the waves breaking over your stern.

Try to avoid rushing down into a trough between wave crests such that your propeller comes out of the water. This results in engine overspeeding and loss of control.

Some power boats are designed with a wide stern and have a tendency to **broach** (turn sideways) in wave troughs after coming down the face of large waves. It is dangerous to go straight down large waves in a small boat as the stern tends to ride high and the propeller come out of the water. This results in the bow digging into the trough and a broach occurring. If you go down the wave at an angle to the trough line, "quartering," you're much better off.

Traveling parallel to the line of waves presents a real hazard in heavy seas. Such a track in wave troughs may result in dangerous rolling of the boat with the very real possibility of swamping or capsizing.

In heavy seas it can be hazardous to turn broadside to large waves.

So stay out of the troughs unless you must change your heading. If you absolutely must turn, take your boat into a trough, throttle back briefly, turn the wheel fully and quickly in the direction you want to go, then apply a sharp burst of power to really scoot around to the new heading.

If you experience engine failure in heavy winds, the **sea anchor** should be deployed from the bow. We recommend having it rigged and connected to the bow eye or cleat before going into severe weather. The sea anchor will exert drag on the bow and keep the boat headed into the wind.

If you are drifting downwind without power, be aware of the dangerous possibility of coming aground on a **lee shore.** If this is a threat, you should be ready to deploy ground tackle, your anchor system, to hold her off the rocks or beach.

While underway in heavy weather, it is vital that you maintain a good lookout at all times. This is particularly true during periods of reduced visibility, and if you are near land.

Wakes

A **wake** is produced astern and to the side of any vessel while underway. It is the water the vessel shoves aside plus the wash off her propeller(s). The wake will move out from the bow and stern at about a 45-degree angle while the vessel is underway. The size and effect of the wake is determined by the size of the vessel and its forward speed. The bigger the boat, and the faster it's going, the bigger the wake.

Wakes are normally treated like waves by the helmsman, but there are several unique situations:

Wakes can be a problem when they intersect with wind-produced waves. This regularly occurs on heavily-used inland lakes as water skiers, personal watercraft operators, and other folks moving at high speeds roar around in every direction. Their wakes, combined with the wind waves, create areas of significant turbulence around the more heavily-used areas.

This can lead to a mighty rough ride as you make your way through disturbed areas. It's normally best to throttle back to avoid the excessive pounding and rough ride in these areas, while maintaining steerageway at all times.

Another situation to watch for is the wake produced in a confined waterway by a vessel moving at high speed. The water displaced by these fast movers can be quite turbulent and spill out into neighboring shallower waters.

When you encounter a fast-approaching boat, reduce your headway and ride out the wake by keeping your bow pointed into it. Although the boater should slow down to avoid giving other boats any problems, don't count on it.

A particularly severe wake can be produced on many waterways by a **"tow of barges."** This is a column of barges being pushed by a tugboat. These barges look harmless as they slowly move along with only a few feet showing above the water. Their hulls, however, may extend down 6 feet or more into the water.

A major disturbance is therefore created in the water when the barges pass. If you are underway in your small boat and encounter a barge tow coming towards you in the waterway it is best to turn well away from it and reduce headway until it is past your position.

If you are outside the channel, say, fishing close by on the flats, always keep your eye out for any wakes coming your way. Head into them if you think they are severe enough. In any case, enjoy the ride.

Submerged Objects

Submerged objects are of major concern to power boaters in all inland lakes, rivers, and coastal waters. Spring run-offs, for example, can cause problems as the seasonal rains bring down debris of all sorts.

This debris is often submerged just under the surface. It presents a definite hazard to the power boat operator for some days or weeks after its arrival in your waterway. The main problem is the damage such debris will do to your hull and engine when you try to run through the stuff.

The best way to move through these areas is at greatly reduced **headway,** keeping a good lookout. This will probably eliminate any significant damage to your hull as you just shove your way through the stuff. Your propeller, however, could take a hit, but that should be of little real concern if you've got the appropriate tools and equipment aboard to change out the shear pin, or put on a replacement propeller.

Other submerged objects include fishing nets, cables, pipelines, boat wrecks, abandoned piers, pilings, wrecked automobiles, and the kitchen sink. So keep a real close watch for anything unusual in the water. Get information from other boaters, and look at the charts of your waterways for areas where drifting stuff might accumulate. Watch for any posted warnings about submerged pipelines or cables.

Shallow Water

There are natural underwater obstructions, such as shoals, reefs, and other areas, that will interfere with the free passage of your boat. Their whereabouts are usually determined by visual observation, reference to nautical or fishing charts, and by talking with folks who know the water.

In most inland bodies of water, both natural and man-made, the lay of the land under the water is usually identical with that around it. So if you see a shoreline sloping into the water, it is very likely that the same slope will be continued underwater.

There is a situation on some inland waters, and many coastal areas, where the water depth varies as a result of tides, both moon and wind-induced, water levels, or other conditions, such as dams opening and closing.

As it is important to know how much water you have beneath your hull, we recommend that all power boaters, except for those operating the smallest of boats on the smallest of waters, install a **depth-sounding device.** This relatively inexpensive instrument will give you a good idea of what is under your boat at any time. Ask your boat dealer to explain these effective devices.

Congestion

There is a medium-sized lake in South Texas that has an amazing collection of watercraft of every size and type. These include rowboats, canoes, sailboats, jet skis, jet-driven personal watercraft, seaplanes (no fooling), runabouts, cruisers, center consoles, and several racing boats with humongous engines.

Puttering around the edges of the lake, and zooming off at high speed to certain secret locations, are the many bass boats. You know the ones: 150-plus HP outboards shoving flat, maroon metallic flake hulls, operated by grim guys with baseball caps turned backwards, all desperately looking for Old Lunker before the sun goes down.

A pleasant weekend brings all these folks out to that lake. Now this is great, but there is a real congestion problem out there as increasing numbers of fun-seeking people simultaneously attempt to use the same water.

This results in jams that look like rush hour in Los Angeles. Conditions are worsened where recreational boating tends to be largely unregulated. There are the Rules of the Road, to be sure, plus local laws and regulations, but many folks just don't seem to know or care about these.

Mix that indifference with the natural high that boating gives, plus the booze, swollen egos, youthful swagger, and pulsing libidos, all cranked onto the same body of water at the same time. It makes the Coast Guard, Corps of Engineers, local sheriff, police, water wardens, whoever, want to call out the Reserves. There really isn't any slick solution for all this, except to do your boating at some other place or time. If that isn't what you can do, then you have to develop defensive techniques to keep you and your boat intact.

One of the best first steps is to *keep a good lookout* at all times while underway. Keep your head out of the cock-

Figure 18. *Danforth Type Anchor and Chain.* This shows a typical Danforth-type anchor with 6 feet of anchor chain. Note that the chain is plastic-coated to lessen the possibility of damage to the boat when hauled over the side, and to help reduce the clanking.

pit. If you see a problem developing, take prompt action to avoid it. Turn away and avert the problem. If you assume that the other guy doesn't know what he's doing, doesn't see you, and doesn't give a damn, a lot of difficulty will be avoided. It's like driving on a busy expressway at rush hour. Maybe we should call it **"Defensive Boating."**

Docking

This maneuver is performed regularly by all boaters, and the techniques must be well learned. There is some resemblance to parking a car here, but the differences far outnumber the similarities. *Always keep in mind that your boat's movements are being controlled by the thrust of the engine, the wind, and the water's current and wave effects.*

Before you attempt to dock, you should be aware of the speed and direction of the wind, and any water currents around the dock. You must also be alert to other boat traffic, swimmers, fishermen, and anything else that might interfere with your docking process.

As you approach the dock, you should be moving at no-wake speed. Pick out the exact spot on the dock where you want to tie up. It is usually best if you can move into this spot running into the wind or current. Note, however, that sometimes this is not possible, and down or crosswind landings are necessary.

As you make your approach, deploy the fenders on the dock side of your boat, as well as making ready the bow and stern mooring lines. Slowly advance toward the dock with enough power to have the boat under complete control. Then, based on the wind and current, go to Neutral when you have just enough headway to reach the dock without further power. Use the engine as necessary to ease her to the spot you picked. It works well if you can approach the dock at about a 20-degree angle, turning parallel to it just as you arrive.

As the boat moves parallel to the dock, your headway should just about be bled off. The boat may pause for a moment as the prevailing wind starts to take her. The mooring lines should be secured to the dock, and the engine shut down at that pause. Check to make certain your fenders prevent the boat from contacting the dock.

Maneuvering practice at slow speeds can be most useful in getting the feel of your boat for the docking process. It's particularly important to be able to handle your boat well when in Reverse. As your skills improve, you will be able to "walk" your boat sideways into the dock using your throttle, wheel, and good judgment.

There are several techniques involving **spring lines** (dock lines) to control the bow and stern of your boat in a variety of very useful ways. Their use around docks and slips can be extremely effective. We recommend that you request information on using spring lines where you dock your boat.

Anchoring

The **ground tackle** (your boat's anchor system) is designed to hold her where you park her under almost any conditions. It is composed of the anchor, line, chain, swivels, and shackles.

The anchor line, with chain, is called the **"rode."** The anchor line connects the anchor chain, and everything else, to the bow eye, or bow cleat, of your boat.

You will also hear about **"scope."** This can be thought of as the total amount of rode you have out when your anchor system is in use. Some more technically-inclined folks may identify the scope as the ratio between the total length of deployed rode and the vertical distance between

Figure 19. *Buoy in Harbor.* When you see this buoy around the marina harbor, you should slow down to "no-wake" speed. The reason for this is to avoid damage to docked boats from wakes caused by speeders.

the bow eye or bow cleat of your boat and the bottom of the body of water you're on.

The length of scope you need varies on how and where your boat is used. Ratios of 10 to 5 times the depth of the water you anchor in are common, dependent on the type of anchor, winds, sea conditions, and type and size of boat. Under average conditions, a scope of 7 to 1 is common.

The **anchor chain** connects directly to the anchor ring, or to a shackle. The chain's weight helps the anchor lie flatter on the bottom so its **flukes,** which are the flat protuberances at the end of the anchor arms, can dig in better. Usually, the larger the anchor, the more chain will be used.

There are many different makes, models, and types of anchors, each designed for particular tasks. Originally, all anchors were made to hold by their massiveness and weight. The newer models utilize certain design features that provide great holding power with reduced weight.

The Danforth anchor is an excellent choice for many small boats. It is named after R.S. Danforth, who introduced the design to the U.S. Navy just prior to World War II. The Danforth is relatively inexpensive, and most effective in sand and mud bottoms. It should be used with some caution on rocky or weedy bottoms. It is not good at resetting itself when dislodged.

The Bruce-type anchor is another good, general-purpose anchor with no moving parts. Other types include the Fisherman, the Pivoting Plow, the Delta, and others designed for special purposes.

It is good practice on many boats to carry two anchors, separately rigged, and capable of being used simultaneously. Their use depends on how and where you use your boat, and under what conditions. If you have questions, we recommend that you seek assistance from a qualified person in your area in selecting the anchor system best suited for your operations.

Most **anchor line** is made of nylon, either braided or in a two- or three-strand twist. Nylon's greatest advantage in this application is its elasticity. This is particularly important considering the heavy, snatching loads exerted on the ground tackle under high wind, current, and wave conditions. Nylon lines can stretch more than one-third of their unstressed length, providing very efficient built-in shock absorbers.

Anchoring techniques must be learned and practiced. You can get away with not using your anchor system properly if you only frequent small waters in good weather. If you use your boat in larger waters, knowing how to use your anchor system effectively will avoid damage and danger to you, your passengers, and your boat.

WARNING

Anchoring a small boat by its stern can be dangerous. The transom on most such boats is usually squared off and has much less freeboard than the bow. Swamping can occur in a strong current, or under heavy wave action, if the anchor line is secured to the stern. Use the bow eye or bow cleat.

Deploying Your Anchor

Let's briefly run through how a single anchor would be put into use:

Free up the anchor and its rode from their respective storage locations. Make sure the rode is not tangled. Then fasten it to the anchor. Secure the **bitter end** (the end in the boat) of the rode to a port or starboard bow cleat. Clear the deck around the anchor and rode of any other items.

After you decide where you want to anchor the boat, go a short way downwind from that spot. Swing around and come back to the spot directly into the wind. As you approach your spot, bring the boat to a stop. Now lower the anchor to bottom. *Do not heave it.* As the boat drifts back with the wind, let out the rode. If necessary, start the engine and slowly back away as the rode leaves the boat.

When you have the desired scope, secure the anchor line to the centerline bow cleat or bow eye. Now you can release the bitter end. Continue slowly backing the boat up until the anchor digs into the bottom and halts the boat. Give the anchor a good pull with your hands. If it doesn't hold, keep repeating the process until the anchor feels solid when you pull it. Now look out both sides of the boat and pick out some landscape or seascape features. Note how they look with respect to your position. This will be useful later to indicate whether you've moved, due to wind or current, from your original position .

When it's time to go, the anchor is returned to the boat in the reverse of its deployment as follows:

The boat will be downwind from the anchor. Start the engine and slowly move forward, bringing in the rode as you proceed. When you are directly over the anchor, pull it straight up and into the boat. You may want to slosh the mud and debris off the anchor before you bring it over the side. If you can't get the anchor released, keep moving the boat straight ahead so that the rode is now pulling on the anchor from the opposite direction. If the anchor still doesn't release, circling around while keeping tension on the rode will usually free it.

Aids to Navigation

Navigational Aids are placed along the coasts and in navigable waters as guides to mark safe water for boat passages. These aids also assist mariners in determining their position in relation to land, and in identifying the location of hidden dangers. Each aid to navigation is designed to provide specific information to the knowledgeable mariner.

These unique sets of navigational markers are made up of various colors, shapes, numbers, letters, and/or lights. They are formally known as the **Lateral System of Buoyage.** This system is maintained by the U.S. Coast Guard either through contract services, or by using assigned personnel. Helmsmen using navigable waters are responsible for understanding and obeying **Navigational Aids.** Helmsmen should also be aware that these aids are subject to being moved due to storms, water currents, collisions, and other actions. Accordingly, they should always be used as "aids," and not infallible markers.

Know also that it is illegal, and possibly dangerous, to tie up to a navigation aid while you go fishing or enjoy a cooling swim. Remember, it is illegal to move, or otherwise tamper with, any Navigational Aid. Don't touch those things!

Several Navigational Aids are usually used together to form a local system that helps mariners follow natural and improved channels. Such aids also provide a continuous system of charted **"marks"** for coastal piloting. Individual Navigational Aids are also used to mark landfalls from seaward and to mark isolated dangers.

"Lateral marks" are buoys or beacons that indicate the port and starboard sides of routes to be followed. Virtually all U.S. lateral marks follow the traditional 3R Rule of "red, right, returning." This means, when returning from sea, or from some other designated direction, keep the red marks on the starboard side of your vessel as you proceed on the waterway.

Please note, however, that the 3R Rule may not be applicable in every situation. Always check it out for the waterways in which you'll be operating.

This Federally maintained Lateral System of Buoyage has been largely standardized, and each state must now comply. This takes some of the guesswork out of navigation.

Contact the Coast Guard Hotline at 1-800-368-5647 for further information on the Lateral System of Buoyage.

Various states have waterway-marking systems that are used in conjunction with the Federal Lateral System of Buoyage. Boaters should contact their State Boating Office to obtain that information for their state.

Navigation Rules

The **Navigation Rules** establish actions to be taken by vessels to avoid collision. The Rules are divided into Inland and International.

Contact the Coast Guard Boating Safety Hotline at 1-800-368-5647 to obtain further valuable information on the Navigation Rules.

The Inland Rules apply to all vessels operating inside the demarcation lines separating inland and international waters. These demarcation lines appear on most charts, and are published in the Navigation Rules. We will highlight several elements of the Inland Rules which apply to all vessels on the inland waters of the United States.

As the possibility of collisions increase when vessels are crossing, meeting, or overtaking, we will emphasize these events.

In crossing situations, the vessel approaching from the starboard side has the right-of-way. At night, for instance, if you see the red, portside light of an approaching vessel, you will know it is coming from your starboard and has the right-of-way. You, as the **give-way vessel,** must turn to your starboard to pass well behind the **stand-on vessel** (the one having the right-of-way). Each vessel is to sound a one-second blast on its horn.

In meeting head-on or nearly so, vessels usually pass portside-to-portside. In a portside passing, each vessel alters course to its starboard, staying well clear of the other in order to permit a safe passage. One short blast is sounded by each boat.

Starboard-to-starboard passing is permitted if the situation warrants. Then each vessel alters course to its port, staying well clear, and each sounds two short horn blasts.

In overtaking situations, the give-way vessel (the overtaker) may pass on either side of the stand-on (the overtaken) vessel. If the overtaker intends to pass on the starboard of the stand-on vessel, he sounds one short blast and moves ahead, keeping well clear of the other vessel. If he intends to pass on the port, two short blasts are sounded and he moves ahead, keeping clear. In both cases the overtaken vessel responds to the overtaker with the same number of short horn blasts.

Generally, less maneuverable vessels have the right-of-way over the more maneuverable. Thus a sailboat, or rowboat, or the Love Boat has the right-of-way over your power boat, as these vessels are a lot less maneuverable.

You generally want to keep to starboard while underway. On narrow winding rivers, it's good to sound your horn with one long blast when you approach a bend you can't see around. If you hear a long blast on the river, and you are heading in that direction, respond with a long blast and head over to starboard as far as possible.

If you are going to enter a designated channel or waterway, vessels underway on that channel have the right-of-way.

The main purpose of the Rules of the Road is to prevent collision accidents while afloat. They should be applied with common sense and consideration for other boaters.

Copies of fully illustrated Rules of the Road may be obtained from the Superintendent of Documents, U.S. Government Printing Office, Washington, DC 20402.

Night Boating

When darkness comes and the familiar daytime landmarks fade, a fascinating world awaits the boater. Night boating can be a most enjoyable experience given reasonably good weather, a properly equipped boat, and adequate advance planning.

It is important that your boat be equipped with the proper **navigation lights.** Most new boats, as delivered by dealers, are so equipped. But verify that fact for your boat before you launch.

*The U.S. Coast Guard provides excellent free publications which will fully describe navigation lights for all size vessels. Call the **Boating Safety Hotline** at **1-800-368-5647.***

Vessels must display their navigation lights between sunset and sunrise, and during other periods of reduced visibility. You should become familiar with the lighting configurations (called **"shapes"**) seen on the various sizes and types of vessels. These can tell you what type the vessels are, and if underway, the direction they are traveling.

Good **night vision** is essential to safe operations when the sun goes down. Your eyes will gradually become accustomed to the darkness if you do not expose them to white light. Your night vision can be impaired if somebody shines a flashlight in your face, or lights a pipe.

Another aspect of night vision is the fact that if you gaze directly at something, you will not see it as well as if you look slightly to one side. This is not a vision flaw, but due to the way your eyes are built.

The planning for your night voyage is important. If you're only going to sneak off to the end of your home lake to catch a few bass after sundown, that's one thing. If you want to launch at midnight, say, in Corpus Christi Bay, and take the Intracoastal Waterway over to Houston, that's another matter entirely. You should plan this type of trip in detail. Use the appropriate marine charts and plot each course leg. Your plan should include all compass headings, way points, navigation aids, weather info, and any other information needed for your comfort and safety.

Information on how to navigate safely at night, or in adverse weather, is best learned in a formal program, or in the company of an experienced helmsman. Failure to plan in detail for any voyage, but particularly in reduced visibility, either at night or in bad weather, is asking for inconvenience at best, and big-time trouble at the worst.

Float Plan

If you depart for more than one day, you should write down a **Float Plan** and give it to some reliable person. If you will be gone for only a few hours, then tell your Float Plan to that reliable person.

Your Float Plan should include where you are going, when you expect to return, and who is going with you. You should include a description of your boat, your tow vehicle, and where it will be parked while you are away. The purpose of all this is to make it possible to rescue you if you don't return when you said you would.

Weather

Weather plays a key role in boating. For your own safety, and that of your passengers, you must be aware of the existing and forecast weather for the areas you will be frequenting. A short outing on local waters may only require a quick look out the window and the TV forecast for your area. More extensive trips, however, require that you be fully aware of the forecast conditions en route and at your destination. You don't want to load and fuel your boat for a long trip and then find out that weather conditions may make it unsafe.

A responsible Skipper will always keep abreast of changing weather conditions. He will never leave the dock when small craft advisories are posted without being fully aware of the conditions to be encountered and his own capabilities.

The **National Oceanic and Atmospheric Administration (NOAA),** of the U.S. Department of Commerce, transmits weather forecasts and issues **Small Craft Advisories. NOAA Weather Radio** provides continuous broadcasts of the latest weather information on one of seven FM frequencies ranging from 162.40 to 162.55 MHz. While these frequencies are not found on the typical home radio, low cost "weather" radios are available from companies such as Radio Shack. These NOAA broadcasts are also received by most good-quality, marine VHF radios.

The **National Weather Service (NWS)** is listed in the telephone directory under the U.S. Department of Commerce. Call NWS for boating forecasts if the NOAA information is not adequate. The NWS also provides Coastal Warnings and Forecasts, Offshore Warnings and Forecasts, High Seas Warnings and Forecasts, Coastal Flood Watches and Warnings, Tropical Storm Advisories, and Tsunami Warnings. **"Tsunamis"** are sea waves caused by underseas disturbances such as earthquakes and landslides.

The NWS Office in Cleveland, Ohio disseminates **Great Lakes** marine weather information, to include the Twice Daily Synopsis, Storm Outlook, Storm Summary, and Great Lakes Ice Freeze-up/Break-up Outlooks.

Your Boat

It's important that your boat be **shipshape,** and ready for the uses you intend. Always take a careful look around and make sure everything is OK before you before you cast off. It is much better to find a problem in the parking lot, or at the dock, than 20 miles out in rising winds.

Checklist

If you have a new, or unfamiliar, boat you may want to develop a **checklist.** Such a list can save you a lot of aggravation until you get well acquainted with your boat and its equipment. Include such things as:

- ⚓ The adequacy of the fuel, oil, and water quantities for the trip planned
- ⚓ Coast Guard-required equipment
- ⚓ Other necessary items, such as sports gear, food and drink, ice, extra clothing, any needed medicines for you or your passengers, glasses and/or sunglasses
- ⚓ First aid kit
- ⚓ Survival gear, as required
- ⚓ Proper loading of the boat: If there is a large amount of cargo to be carried, deduct one person from the boat's capacity for every 150 pounds cargo

⚓ Making sure that everything on board works OK: Actually try all the electronics. Check all the controls and instruments.

⚓ Giving the whole boat a good sniff test for fuel leaks.

CAUTION!

Do not proceed with fuel leaks or fumes present on your boat.

Include in your checklist any other items you need for your particular vessel and personal needs.

Fueling

Gasoline is a remarkable substance, but because it is so familiar, many people have become indifferent to the pure energy in the stuff. Keep in mind that:

⚓ Gasoline evaporates rapidly. Its vapors are heavier than air, and rapidly seek the lowest points in your boat.

⚓ A vaporized mixture of about 14 parts air to 1 part of gasoline is highly explosive, and, on combustion, releases more energy than a like amount of dynamite.

⚓ Most boat explosions occur shortly after refueling, due primarily to gasoline spills.

⚓ Your job as Skipper is to keep gasoline vapor out of your boat to the maximum extent possible, and to eliminate any unshielded ignition sources when gasoline vapor may be present.

Check with your Owner's Manual or your dealer to determine the proper fuels and oils to be used. It is essential that only the specified fuel be utilized. Failure to do so can result in serious damage to your engine.

We believe that unleaded automotive gasoline with a 97 anti-knock index (AKI) is the lowest acceptable AKI for most marine engines. Again, your Owner's Manual should be consulted for your particular engine.

Many gasolines are now routinely blended with alcohol in percentages that vary with the brand, the location, and the time of year. We recommend that you should not use any unleaded gasoline having more than 10 percent ethanol, or 5 percent methanol, even if the fuels contain co-solvents or **corrosion inhibitors.** If these fuels are used, there could well be increased deterioration in fuel hoses and other parts of the system.

We also recommend that you do not fill any gasoline tank aboard your boat more than about 95 percent full, to avoid fuel's being vented as the ambient temperature rises. In some locations, however, it is common practice to fill fuel tanks to a nearly full level to avoid condensation problems. Please check with your local U.S. Power Squadron, or Coast Guard Auxiliary unit, on this matter for your vessel.

Portable Fuel Tanks

Fill these tanks away from your boat to eliminate the possibility of spills on board and to have more room to handle the tanks.

When filling, make certain that the fuel hose nozzle makes and keeps a metal-to-metal contact with the tank filler neck. This is to prevent static electricity sparking, which can cause an explosion. Start by putting in about a gallon of gasoline. Now add all the oil required, and shake the tank well. Next add the rest of the gasoline. Replace the cap, wipe the tank down to remove any spilled gasoline or oil, and return it to the boat. Never pour the oil directly into an empty tank and then put in all the gasoline. It will not mix right.

Built-in Tanks

Filling these is much like putting fuel in your automobile's tank, but there are certain safety procedures which should be followed:

If afloat, moor your boat securely at the fuel point. Then turn off the boat's electrical system, disembark all passengers, close all hatches and ports, put out any open flames, smoking materials, and any other source of ignition. Do a **sniff test** around your vessel. If you can smell fuel strongly, do not service your tanks until you find and correct that leak.

If available, connect the gas pump grounding lines to the boat. Insert the fuel hose nozzle into your tank's filler neck, making certain there is metal-to-metal contact between the filler neck and hose nozzle. Now pump the fuel to no more than about 95 percent full to prevent spillage.

When done, replace the fuel cap(s), and wipe down any spills. Open all hatches, turn on the bilge blower and let it run for several minutes. Now give your boat another good sniff test for any gasoline fumes. Check the bilge and other low areas carefully. If no trace of fumes is detected, you can safely start your engine and shove off. If fumes are present, continue ventilating until cleared.

CAUTION!

Do not start your engine if gasoline fumes are present in your boat.

If you are servicing your boat on its trailer in a gas station, refuel as you would while afloat. Be sure to continuously hold the fuel nozzle against the tank's filler neck to avoid static electricity sparking.

As other people may be close by, be alert to their smoking, particularly while you are pumping fuel into the boat. Ask them to please back off if they get close with lit tobacco. Your day would probably not be filled with joy if your boat blew up right there at the gas pump.

On a more pleasant note, you should check with your State Comptroller's office to see if you are entitled to a refund of the tax you pay for each gallon of gasoline used in your boat. This is the case in Texas, and it amounts to about a 20¢-per-gallon refund. This reimbursement is allowed because a boat is not a road vehicle, and state fuel tax receipts are largely used for the upkeep of the state road system. You must, of course, keep all your receipts to back up your claims for reimbursement.

Big-Water Boating

This special section was provided by Captain Paul W. Eccleston, professional guide and waterman, of Corpus Christi, Texas.

When you decide to take your trailered boat to the big water, there are a few considerations you must give to safety and comfort in order to better enjoy and survive your day. It is important to recognize that big-water boating can present a vastly different operating environment than smaller waters.

"Big water" here means any body of water where you can go **"off-shore"** beyond view of land. So if you plan on doing any boating in the Atlantic, Pacific, or Gulf of Mexico coastal waters, on the Great Lakes, or on any other good-sized inland lake, you are on big water, and should listen up good here.

Boat Characteristics

Your boat should be a deep-V or modified-V hull design, or some variation thereof. Flat-bottom, pontoon, and most tri-hulls are not generally suited for safe big-water use.

Before you take your boat off-shore, you must know something about that boat. These things will become obvious only after spending some time on your boat in-shore.

You need to become well acquainted with the trim of the boat and how well it can be controlled in various sea conditions. Any roll, pitch, or yaw will become more exaggerated in the wave action of the open sea. You should learn about your boat's characteristics in-shore, not off-shore.

Fuel Management

In the course of your in-shore "try-outs" you should get a good estimate of your boat's fuel consumption in average gallons per hour, at various speeds, as well as its average miles per gallon. This can be done the easiest by completely filling your tank at the beginning of a day's outing. Then, after you've finished for the day, completely fill that tank again. The amount of fuel you add after the day's run is what you used that day. Assume you added 30 gallons of fuel after you ran that tank for 3 hours. Then 30 gallons divided by 3 hours gives you a 10 gallons per hour fuel consumption rate.

Next, estimate your distance traveled in miles that day. This can be done by plotting your course on a nautical chart of the area, or by traveling over some known distances. Then, knowing the gallons of fuel you added, calculate miles per gallon. Say the 90 miles you traveled used 30 gallons of gas. This gives you a 3 miles per gallon fuel consumption rate.

With this information, you can now calculate your boat's range in miles and allowable running time. These are extremely important figures that you must have to safely proceed off-shore. *Please note, however, that these computed rates are approximations.* They will vary greatly as a result of engine, weather, and sea conditions. Here's all that in formula form:

Range in Miles = (miles/gallon consumption rate) × (fuel tank capacity). In our example:

Range = (miles/gallon is 3) × (assume a fuel tank capacity of 40 gallons) gives you a round trip range of 120 miles.

Running Time in Hours = (total gallons in tank) ÷ (gallon/hour consumption rate). In our example:

Running time = (total gallons in tank is 40) ÷ (gallons/per hour of 10) gives you running time of 4 hours on the full tank of 40 gallons.

After these calculation are made, subtract 10 percent for an in-shore safety margin. Then subtract 20 percent for the off-shore safety margin.

Dead Reckoning

Many times you will have a need to estimate your **distance traveled,** and the other factors of **speed** and **time,** without the aid of buoys, channel markers, or other navigation aids. The method used to do this is called **Dead Reckoning.**

Use the following formula:

Distance Traveled = (Rate) × (Time). Thus your speed of 20 MPH over a two-hour en route time will move you 40 miles.

You might remember all this from an early high school math class as Distance = Rate × Time or (D = RT). With this, you can easily calculate any one of the three variables if you know the other two.

Weather and Sea Conditions

The biggest difference between boating on in-shore bays and lakes versus off-shore waters is the weather. You are at the mercy of the weather at all times while off-shore.

You should always listen to NOAA weather broadcasts before you leave safe harbor. However, you must learn to always combine the NOAA forecasts with local conditions reported by other boats already on the water.

These include day cruisers, sport fishermen, local oil company boats, commercial fishing and shrimping boats, and "party" fishing boats. You will note that many times actual conditions vary greatly from the NOAA or local TV station reports.

Listen Up, Now!

In general, a boat that rides on a trailer need not be leaving port in seas greater than 5 feet and choppy. A 5-foot swell is quite comfortable, but put a big water chop on it and it becomes formidable. Remember, even though you can run your boat in 5 feet of rough water, a sudden squall can make it a lot worse. So before you leave, consider how much fun you're going to have if it gets worse.

If you do get caught in very heavy weather, try to keep your bow heading into the sea. To prevent capsizing, proceed slowly and be ready to use power to go through the waves. *Don't let the sea control you.* If you lose power, be ready to deploy your sea anchor, a type of sea-going parachute that will keep the boat headed into the sea when attached to your bow eye. If conditions have caused you to lose control of your boat, you should contact the Coast Guard on VHF Channel 16. If you feel that lives are at risk, you should begin your transmission with MAYDAY.

Remember though, that if you are having problems because of weather, it is likely that others in your area are also having trouble for the same reason, so don't expect help immediately. This brings us back to your weather considerations before deciding to leave port. Think about it. Are you really prepared? Is the boat seaworthy enough? If you have any doubts, you should abort your voyage.

Remember, *you should own a boat for the sheer fun of it.* If you take things slow and easy and consult with local experts (charter boat captains, fishing guides, oil company boat captains, etc.), you will build a foundation for a safe and fun experience that you and your family and friends will enjoy for years. You will begin to realize what "ship-shape" really means, and why strict discipline in maintaining and operating your boat is so important.

> *Life on the water has made me a better man by teaching self-discipline, decision-making, safety, patience, and appreciation of the strength and beauty of the sea.*
>
> Captain Paul W. Eccleston.

AUTHOR'S NOTE

Captain Paul W. Eccleston, USCG License #276412, is a highly skilled, professional fishing and waterfowl hunting guide. He operates both off-shore and in the many bays of the Texas Coastal Bend. Write Paul at 4165 Eagle, Corpus Christi, TX 78413, or call him at (512) 853-2713 for more information, and to set up a really great trip.

NOTES

NOTES

Chapter 5

~~~~~~

Maintaining Your Rig— Avoid Those Breakdowns

> *This chapter provides you with key service tips for your trailer, boat, and engine.*

This chapter is for every boater from the hard driving, run-it-till-it-breaks Skipper to the marina socialite. We give you some proven ideas that will help prevent those really frustrating breakdowns on the water and the highway.

At the other extreme are those good people who consider caring for their rig more fun than anything. The social life around the marina or launch ramp while they're polishing and lubricating is about all the boating they want.

Your Boat Trailer

It is important that your trailer be properly set up for your boat. This means that the various parts of the trailer must be adjusted and positioned for your particular boat. This is normally done by your dealer when you buy a new boat. Many folks, however, buy their trailer boats from other individuals, and just can't be certain that everything is set up right. In any case, it would be wise for you to check your rig now to make sure that:

⚓ The stern of your boat does not overhang the trailer supports when the bow is snug against the bow stop

⚓ The boat is centered on the trailer's supports

⚓ The boat is fully supported by the trailer's supports over the full length of its hull

If your boat will not sit properly on its trailer, you should see a boat service facility and have that problem corrected. Operating a trailer with an improperly positioned boat can cause major structural damage to the boat's hull.

Most other trailer problems come from the **wheels and hubs, brakes, electrical system,** and **coupler.** Let's now look at these.

Wheels and Hubs

These take about the hardest beating of any part of your trailer. They run under a load at high speeds on the highway, get good and warm, and then get dunked in cold water. Then they sit for awhile, then back in the cold water again, and back on the highway. This could well be repeated several times in a day.

The three main areas of concern on the wheels are **loose lug nuts or wheel bolts, improper tire pressure,** and **lack of wheel bearing lubrication.**

The following recommendations will help:

Keep your trailer's lug nuts or wheel bolts firmly snugged down. If one or more loosen up while underway, you could lose that wheel. Ask a tire or boat dealer to show you the proper tightness of the wheel lug nuts or bolts, if you aren't sure.

If you notice any missing lug nuts or bolts, replace them immediately with an exact match of the original.

Your trailer's tires must be properly inflated. The most common cause for trailer-tire problems is under-inflation. Check each tire's pressure when it's cold, before you move

Figure 20. *Boat Trailer Wheel.* This shows a BEARING BUDDY installed on the hub of a trailer wheel. Note nipple fitting where you use a hand-operated grease gun to force waterproof grease into the spring-loaded hub. The positive pressure in the hub keeps the grease in and the water out.

your rig. Thirty-five pounds is typical for most tires on a single-axle trailer. Check with your boat dealer if you have more than one axle.

We use a small, 12-volt powered **air compressor** that stays in the tow vehicle to inflate low tires, air mattresses, and water toys. A friend keeps one of those **portable air tanks** in his tow vehicle for these purposes.

Check your tires for cuts and gouges. If you can see the tire fabric in a cut or gouge, that tire should be replaced. In the meantime, put your spare on in place of that cut tire.

If you have a hard time getting that spare wheel off its carrier, remember in the future to regularly coat the threads of retaining nuts or bolts with marine grease.

By the way, you *do* have a spare tire, don't you?

When your trailer's tires need to be replaced, make sure you get the right type for your rig. Buy quality tires and you won't be broken down alongside the road some dark and stormy night. Ask a qualified tire shop to give you some replacement options for your make and model of trailer.

Regularly check your trailer wheel rims for corrosion. Excessively corroded rims can result in bead separation and premature failure of tubeless tires. Some boaters put tubes in their tubeless trailer tires and eliminate that problem, particularly if they operate around salt water.

Do you carry a **jack** that will safely lift and support your loaded trailer? Did you know that many automobile jacks are not constructed to safely lift your trailer? Check yours out. If it doesn't lift your trailer correctly, get one that does before you go on the road with your rig.

Do you have a lug wrench that fits your trailer's lug nuts or bolts? Many automobile lug wrenches will not fit trailer lug nuts, so you may need to get one that does. Check it out.

If your trailer's **wheel bearings** are properly lubricated you will eliminate one of the main causes of highway breakdowns. We recommend that your trailer be equipped with the **BEARING BUDDY** product, or something similar. These simple devices replace the dust cap on the wheel hub. They allow grease to be pumped into the hub through a nipple fitting. The positive pressure induced by a plunger and spring keeps water out and the bearings (and you) rolling. Wheel hubs should be pumped up after each trip with a hand-operated grease gun.

We recommend that your **wheel hubs** be inspected at least annually by a competent technician. Any less-than-serviceable components should be replaced. Don't fool with this. Better do it now in comfort than by the side of the road later.

If you put your trailer boat rig into storage for the winter season, you should jack up the trailer and put jack stands under the axle(s). This takes the weight off the trailer's tires and springs, thus prolonging their life.

The winter season is also a good time to do minor maintenance on the trailer to help get it in shape for spring. This would include rust removal, spot painting, replacement of the winch line or strap, wiring system repairs, cleaning and lubrication, and the like.

Trailer Brakes

It's the law in many states that brakes are required if your trailer's **Gross Vehicle Weight Rating (GVWR)** is more than 1,500 pounds. Check with your **state Motor Vehicle Division** to make sure your trailer is in compliance.

Many boat trailers have **"surge" brakes** that function independently of the tow vehicle braking system. The principle is quite simple. As the tow vehicle slows down, the trailer's master brake cylinder activates. This, in turn, causes the trailer's brakes to be activated through its hydraulic system.

Trailer brake systems need to be regularly inspected for wear, and any compensating adjustments made. During these inspections, worn or broken components must be replaced. Operating a rig with improperly functioning trailer brakes is dangerous.

Trailer Electrical System

The **trailer electrical system** can be a persistent source of problems unless certain preventive measures are taken regularly.

This system is usually quite simple and readily serviced. Problems are usually related to grounding caused by corrosion and wear in and around the light fixtures and in the wiring. These groundings are caused by bad connectors and/or worn insulation.

A little time taken in understanding your trailer's electrical system will pay you big future dividends. Here are some preventive tips to help you keep rolling:

Every six months or so (monthly if you are operating around salt water) check both your tow vehicle's trailer circuit and your trailer's wiring system. Look for faulty insulation, bare wires, badly corroded connectors, etc. Tape up, or use liquid neoprene insulation, as required. Replace corroded connectors and terminals.

Inspect all trailer light fixtures. If you see corrosion around and/or inside a fixture, it should either be taken apart, thoroughly cleaned and sprayed with a silicon lubricant, or else changed out.

Do not operate your trailer with inoperative light fixtures. This applies to both daylight as well as night-time operations. Aside from keeping you on the right side of the law, trailer lights that work will save you much hassle. Attempting turns or stops in traffic, for example, without working turn signals or brake lights, is asking for trouble.

You may get away with the bad lights for a while, but eventually somebody will slam into your rig and then claim that you didn't signal properly, or that they didn't see you. Or the police will notice the error of your ways and slap you with a ticket. Either way, it's much cheaper and safer to keep your lights working properly.

Coupler

The trailer's **coupler,** and the tow vehicle's ball hitch, form the all-important connecting link between the two. Make certain that your coupler and ball hitch are of the same size and properly installed on the trailer and tow vehicle.

It is important that you check that coupler before you make a hook-up with your tow vehicle. Look for any sign of damage to its body and remove any foreign material inside the ball socket. The latch mechanism and the ball clamp inside the ball socket should move freely.

Occasionally the coupler may be subject to unusual torsional stresses due to uneven road or launch ramp conditions, and become deformed. The coupler appears to be twisted, rather than "looking" straight ahead. This can cause the ball clamp to be jammed against the coupler's side and not functioning properly. *Have the coupler repaired or replaced if you note this damage.* Such repairs are relatively simple and inexpensive.

> *It is dangerous to operate your trailer if the coupler's ball clamp does not fully engage the ball and the latch mechanism is not completely down and locked.*

After you inspect the coupler, check the **safety chains** to make sure they are securely fastened to the coupler and that connecting hooks are intact. *Never* operate your rig without the safety chains being properly in place.

Trailer Kit

Over the years, we've assembled a useful "kit" containing items that have been real **get-home insurance.** The kit stays in the tow vehicle where it is easily accessible. The following items have proven very useful at various times over the years:

- ⚓ Small air compressor—12-volt, with about 6 feet of air hose, chuck, and enough wire to reach from your tow vehicle's power source (usually the cigarette lighter socket) to the back of the trailer.
- ⚓ Flashlights, metal construction—2
- ⚓ Hand-operated grease gun filled with water-proof lithium grease.
- ⚓ Trailer jack
- ⚓ Trailer wheel lug wrench
- ⚓ Wheel bearings and seals—1 set
- ⚓ Highway flares—12
- ⚓ Assorted light bulbs—1 for each fixture
- ⚓ Combination tail/stop-light fixture
- ⚓ Amber clearance lamp fixture
- ⚓ Fuses for trailer's electrical system—6
- ⚓ Plastic electrical tape
- ⚓ Duct tape
- ⚓ Marine grease in tube
- ⚓ WD-40 spray lubricant
- ⚓ Tire sealer/inflator—4 large size (these last about a year and then should be replaced)
- ⚓ Insulated wire—10 feet or so

These items are kept in two canvas bags purchased at the local surplus store for a few bucks. We use the tow vehicle's hand tools rather than assembling a set just for the trailer. If you don't have a set of tools for your tow vehicle, it would be a good idea to put one together before your next road trip.

We recommend that you learn how to perform the simple repairs that every boat trailer needs from time to time. Find a mechanic to come to your place (or you go over to his) and show you how to change out the wheel bearings and the seals. Then actually do it while the mechanic is there to help. When you get through with the bearings, put on the spare tire. Next, have him show you how to troubleshoot an electrical problem in the trailer's circuits. The ask him if he has any suggestions on things you should do to keep your rig rolling. Pick his brain for as long as it takes you to understand how to troubleshoot your trailer and the tools you need.

The price you pay that mechanic will be returned many, many times over in the future.

Having your Trailer Kit with you, and knowing how to install things, will save you the sky-high repair bills that an away-from-home garage will lay on you for roadside repairs. Not to mention what could be a delay of several days getting back on the road. Certain trailer parts may have to be ordered from a distant wholesaler, or even the factory, and that can take many days, or even weeks.

Your Boat

Keep your boat as clean as possible inside and out. Get hull stains off and out with any good marine cleaner before they have a chance to set.

It is particularly important that you wash your boat with fresh water immediately after each use in salt water.

If you don't have the inclination to do this, hire somebody, but get it done. The price you pay for neglecting this chore is a greatly increased rate of deterioration of your expensive investment. After you get through rinsing the salt off your boat, make sure that you use a chamois or cotton bath towel and wipe off any rinse water remaining on the shiny parts (glass, engine cowling, console, gauges, etc.). Unless this is done, these areas will soon begin to show unsightly spots due to the dissolved minerals in the water.

We have seen these mineral deposits so bad that compounding, the use of a fine abrasive common in automotive paint jobs, was the only way to remove the deposits and the etching they caused.

If you have stains on your boat's **gel coat,** get some OSPHO, or other phosphoric acid solution. Spray it on and let sit until the stain disappears, then rinse. This will not hurt the gel coat, but as it might discolor some adjacent stained or painted surfaces, first test a small area.

If you fish, be careful to get the scales, guts, and dropped bait off decks and other areas as soon as possible, unless you like that rich smell.

Vinyl trim and **upholstery** should be regularly cleaned and protected with any of the vinyl cleaners. This is best done every few weeks to help offset the bleaching effect of sunlight.

Your **glass windshield** should be cleaned with any good commercial glass cleaner. Use toothpaste to help remove minor scratches in the glass.

Plastic windshields and **side panels** are best cleaned with a good commercial plastic cleaner. This can help remove mild scratches and some **crazing** (tiny cracks in random patterns that can cover plastic surfaces).

If your boat is regularly moored in either fresh or salt water, you should consult with your boat dealer, or service facility, about the best methods to keep the bottom clear of **marine growths.** Fresh- and salt-water algae are a constant problem, as are the barnacles present in salt water. Sometimes the boat must be hauled—removed from the water—and these growths removed by a professional using elbow grease and acid.

The application of a **bottom paint** may be helpful. Such a paint *may* help prevent the formation of some marine growths on the submerged portions of your hull. The cost can be high to install and maintain this paint, however. Ask somebody who doesn't sell the paint what would be best for your waters.

Use **marine paste wax** on your fiberglass hull, preferably twice a year. Note that automotive wax is not suitable. It is designed to be used on painted metal surfaces. Marine wax is specially formulated to be used on gel coated fiberglass.

All metal hardware installed aboard your boat should be made of stainless steel, brass, bronze, or aluminum. Stainless steel is best for items carrying a load.

If your boat was built primarily for use in fresh water (ask your dealer, or write or call the manufacturer to find this out), then either:

(a) Don't put that boat in salt water; or,

(b) Change all the bolts and screws to stainless; or,

(c) Be prepared to saw, or drill out and replace, all the original fasteners with stainless steel after they've corroded away.

All electrical connections should be either sealed with a heat shrink tubing, or liquid neoprene, upon installation.

It is a bad practice to access your boat's power source by splicing directly into a live wire. Every time a wire is cut, or insulation penetrated, corrosion will result. This eventually causes a voltage drop, which will result in the malfunction and failure of some electronic component. Access to power should only be obtained at a **fuse block** or panel.

Electrical connections at the battery are vulnerable to corrosion problems. The combination of salt water and battery acid really accelerates the corrosion process. To help prevent this, disconnect all wires from the positive (+) terminal of the battery after each voyage in salt or brackish water.

CAUTION!

Prior to disconnecting battery wires, completely ventilate the boat's battery compartment. Make sure all electronics, lights, engines, etc., are turned off. Devices left switched on will cause a spark at the battery when their wires are lifted off the battery's terminals. Such sparking can be dangerous if there are any vapors present.

If you would rather avoid the inconvenience of disconnecting battery wires, install a master switch on your boat. See your boat service folks for the simple installation.

To help keep your boat's **running lights** working, put a light coating of silicon grease on the base and threads of each bulb, lightly coat the interior of the lamp receptacles with the grease, and spray the lenses with silicone spray.

The Engine

The key to a happy engine is **preventive maintenance** performed according to the engine manufacturer's schedule. This preventive maintenance program is in the Owner's Manual that came with your new engine. If you can't locate the manual, contact a dealer, or order one directly from the manufacturer. The few bucks it costs will be repaid many times over the years.

Ask your boat service folks, if, according to the service bulletins they receive, there is anything else you should be doing for your particular model of engine. As these bulletins are usually not widely publicized outside the service business network, it pays to keep in close contact with your service facility to make sure you know the latest.

Here are some engine tips that will help you have more pleasant voyages.

Carefully look at your engine(s) every time you use your boat. Make sure that everything is where it should be. If something doesn't look, smell, or feel right, either fix it or get it fixed.

Keep your fuel filters clean. If you're running an outboard, keep the fuel line hose and bulb in good shape.

Carry a spare fuel hose and bulb for your outboard. You may not need this often, but when you do it's get-home-insurance.

Down at the bottom of your outboard or I/O is its **lower unit.** You should ensure that its service needs are properly met. This involves periodic draining and refilling with a factory-specified lubricant. Check the fluid drained out for any metal particles or water. If you find either of these conditions, work is needed. See your boat dealer or service facility for help.

After use in salt water, it is a good idea to run fresh water through your outboard and I/O (if it uses outside water for cooling). This helps to clear away salt, and gets out any other debris that may be in the cooling system. Then lift the engine's cowling and lightly wash the engine, but not the carburetors. Let everything dry and then spray with WD-40.

You should regularly service all the engine's grease fittings and check all fluid levels on the tilting, lifting, and steering mechanisms. Consult your Owner's Manual for the recommended time intervals for this, and other periodic service.

If the steering on your outboard is of the mechanical push-pull type, regularly grease the **steering rod** that goes through the engine. Then turn the steering wheel all the way to port when the engine is not in use. This should encase the steering rod inside the engine housing, protecting it from rain and sunlight and keeping it working freely. Do not store an ungreased steering rod in this manner as it may seize and be very hard to free.

Your Owner's Manual should be consulted when you service the engine for winter storage. Proper **winterization** of your engine will protect your expensive investment.

It's important to check out your engine, after it has been in winter storage, before you put it back into regular use. This mainly involves removing any preservatives and reconnecting any disconnected hoses.

We also recommend that you carefully inspect your outboard engine several times each year for proper mounting on your boat's transom. Check to make sure that the engine is solidly mounted and absolutely vertical within about ¼-inch of the boat's centerline. Also check that, for routine use, the boat's cavitation plate is even with the bottom of the boat.

Higher or lower cavitation plate placement, however, can be made to improve boat performance, depending on how you use your boat, and other variables. See your boat dealer for help with this.

If you run an outboard engine manufactured after 1982, you should request your service facility to check the engine's "start-in-gear protection" (SGIP) at least once each year. The SGIP is a safety mechanism inside the outboard engine that allows the engine to start only when the gear shifter position is in Neutral. It normally requires no maintenance; however, use of the engine in salt or brackish water can cause corrosion problems on the SGIP.

Prior to 1982 there were many fatal accidents each year that occurred due to engine starts in Forward or Reverse. Persons were thrown overboard unexpectedly, and in many cases, struck by the boat or the propeller as it surged by. Please have the SGIP checked on your engine.

A ship is ever in need of repairing.

John Taylor, *A Navy of Landships*

NOTES

Chapter 6

~~~~~~

Storing Your Boat Rig—
The Facts You Need

> *This chapter provides you with the facts*
> *you need to make a sound storage decision*
> *for your trailer boat rig.*

Thinking about boat storage pales compared to your happy thoughts about the great days of fun in the sun you're going to enjoy. Yet secure storage for your boat is important, and you must face up to it sooner or later. So let's do it sooner.

There are a large number of places you can store your trailer boat. These range from your driveway to a covered boat stall in some swanky marina. We have found that, in most cases, storage choices are driven by **convenience** and **cost.**

Convenience

The convenience element is important. If it is a real hassle to get your boat on the water, a lot of fun goes out of your boating. Here's an example:

Some years ago, we leased a not-so-cheap stall in a local boat storage facility for a 22-foot runabout. This was done in a hurry and with no real check of the place. As it turned out, the boat stall we were assigned was only about 20 inches wider than the trailer, and the stall door would close only if our boat engine's lower unit was jammed against the back wall. Further, the stall was located in the middle of the back row of a double row of identical stalls.

I was driving a ¾-ton, long-bed pickup at the time, and getting the boat trailer in and out of that little stall on those hot Texas summer afternoons was a real exercise in frustration. Backing into the stall was the worst. There just wasn't enough maneuver room between the rows to snake the big rig into that stall. It usually took several passes before everything lined up right so I could jackknife the rig in without hitting something or somebody.

We fumed around that dumb place for some months. Then after an extremely hot and crowded Labor Day weekend, we said, "Enough is enough," sacrificed the deposit, and moved on down the road to another place where things were a lot more convenient.

Before you sign or pay anything, actually put your boat into the offered stall.

It's also a good idea to rent as large a stall as you can afford. This is not only for the ease-of-access, but also to store all the bulky gear you'll wind up carrying in your boat. You know, the ice chests, air mattresses, inner tubes, knee boards, water skis, and all the other water toys.

It's good to have some place to keep that stuff, so if you want to go fishing, or just cruise around some quiet afternoon, you can do so without having the boat filled with plastic horses and sea dragons.

Closely tied in with the convenience factor is the total cost of your storage facility. These costs can vary widely around most popular waterways, so shop around.

Costs

There are several factors to consider in analyzing the costs of boat storage. The two most significant are the actual **rental** or **lease** fees of the storage facility, and the

transportation cost of getting between your residence, the boat's storage location, and the places where you will use the boat.

Rental and lease costs are usually driven by regional demand and the nature of the facilities and services provided. A stall in an enclosed facility in a crowded urban location, for example, will usually cost a lot more than a parking spot in an open field away from the city.

Always shop around for the best deal. It may take some looking, but good deals are out there. This is important, as storage costs can be a major expenditure over time.

Computing the transportation costs for the round trips between your residence and your rig storage is straightforward. These include fuel and other vehicle costs, plus food, lodging, rest stops, etc., necessary for the trip.

To keep these costs as low as possible, most boaters select a storage location at, or on the way to, the body of water where they do most of their boating. Consider this if you *regularly* travel to a body of water a considerable distance from your home. If you store your rig at home, the total cost of towing the boat back and forth to the water could exceed the cost of your leasing storage space near the water. This is due to the fact that the fuel and other costs of towing an average-size trailer boat are about twice what it costs to operate your tow vehicle alone. This aspect should be considered if maximum economy is important.

Storage Options

While there are many storage possibilities, the discussions which follow cover the most common types of boat storage.

On-the-Trailer Storage

As the name implies, your boat stays on its trailer while in storage.

Your Home

This is usually the cheapest method and is used by most of us, either regularly or periodically. In addition to being easy on your bank account, it's really good to have that rig out there, ready to go. Then, when you get the urge, just hook her up and roll.

To avoid unnecessary problems, check into whether there are any **zoning laws,** ordinances, or other restrictive legislation where you live that would affect the storage of a boat rig. Some communities have enacted such laws but may not enforce them, absent any complaints.

There also may be covenants or deed restrictions prohibiting boats, mobile homes, work trailers, etc. from being stored outside on residential properties. Check your property deed, if you own your place, or with the owner of the property, if you are a renter.

Note also that if you store a boat rig on your premises, there may be an impact on your automobile, marine, and residential fire and liability insurance coverages. Check all your policies carefully, as there are big bucks involved.

Depending on its size, and the availability of space, your rig can be stored in the garage or driveway, or in some other spare space you may have out back. If at all possible, it is best to protect the boat rig from the elements. A carport or similar shelter is good for this.

If you decide to keep your rig inside your garage, you may eliminate most of the problems with unhappy neighbors.

CAUTION!
Flammables should be removed from the boat before you store it in an enclosed space.

There is an immediate danger of explosion and fire if flammable vapors from your boat rig reach any open flame, such as a gas-fired hot-water heater in your garage.

Fighting Boat Theft at Home

The **theft of gear** from your boat is obviously best avoided by keeping valuables elsewhere. Crimes of this type are commonly committed by persons roaming around looking for whatever they can fence quickly.

As said earlier, a simple, high quality, water-resistant **alarm system** on your boat can be very effective against this type of crime. In addition, a tightly fitted **boat cover** is helpful, as it keeps the boat's contents out of sight.

Depending on the layout of your place, it may be effective to brightly illuminate the outside boat storage area after dark. Inexpensive floodlights can be easily installed, and manually operated from inside the house. They also can be controlled by an outside motion and/or light detector. Aim the motion detector so that the neighborhood cats and dogs don't turn on your lights, but a person at the tongue of your trailer would.

You may also want to use an automatic photoelectric device that turns your security lights on after dark and off again when the sun comes up, a clock-driven timer, or some combination of these. These devices, designed for outside use, are available at most large hardware stores.

It can be difficult, however, to adequately safeguard your complete rig against a really determined professional thief. A 5-foot-long bolt cutter will go through most padlocks and chains like a knife through warm butter.

That fancy lock on your trailer's coupler may look unbeatable, but a good boat thief will simply lift the trailer's tongue onto his bumper, tie the coupler down with baling wire, and drive to some quiet place. There he can get it ready for the road by putting a cutting torch to the lock, or just loading the whole stolen rig into a waiting van.

The battle against boat theft is a continuing problem. There really is no one magic solution, but you can slow the thieves down by employing a few common-sense measures. Here are some ideas:

⚓ Consider parking another vehicle in the driveway close to your rig. That vehicle could be stolen too, of course, but if you have safeguarded it with an alarm system or steering wheel restraining device like THE CLUB, an effective deterrent is present.

⚓ Another method is to immobilize the wheels of your trailer. This can be accomplished several ways, depending upon the design of your trailer. There are commercial devices on the market that are useful for wheel immobilization. One such device is similar to the BOOT used by some city police departments to control parking violators.

⚓ Hammerlock Industries, Inc. of Miami, Florida (305-223-6097) manufactures a line of boat trailer anti-theft devices, including their BOOTLOCK. Give them a call, or see your local boat dealer, if you need help in locating a local source for this or similar items.

⚓ If the rig will not be used for a while, you may want to consider removing one of the wheels and storing it inside your garage. Support the trailer axle with a good, solid jack stand while the wheel is off.

NOTE

You can get so paranoid about theft that you lose your sense of humor. You don't want to do that. You must always be alert, however, as thefts happen when you least expect them. Unusual sounds at any time, strangers hanging out or driving around, or anything else that doesn't seem right, should lead you to call the police.

Now let's consider several **commercial boat storage** options.

We want to emphasize the importance of a legally sufficient, written agreement between you, the boat owner, and the owner or agent of any premises where you store your rig. This agreement should clearly spell out all the terms and conditions of storage on those premises. Included should be clear references to the various liabilities and responsibilities involved during the life of the agreement, as well as the various charges that may be incurred as a result of the agreement. The obligations of all parties in any such lease arrangement should be clearly spelled out *before* you put your rig in the facility. Of particular concern should be the responsibilities of the parties in the event there is loss or damage to your property while in that stall, or anywhere else on the premises.

Covered Dry Storage

This is a popular and reasonably inexpensive method to get your boat locked up and out of the weather. You will see these shed-type storage structures around most publicly-used bodies of water. They are erected by

Figure 21. *Covered Boat Storage.* Here are a couple of rows of typical covered storage stalls in a facility in Texas. The rows are about 75 feet apart. As you note, the area is unpaved. You can guess what it's like when the spring and fall rains arrive.

enterprising locals and other entrepreneurs, and satisfy a real need. Their lease or rental cost usually varies with the competition, the services and facilities provided, the time of year you arrive to rent that stall, and the location.

As you evaluate these facilities, make certain there is enough maneuvering room in front of the structure to permit the easy in-and-out of your rig. Remember, actually put your rig in that stall a few times before you sign anything. As you may discover, what looks like a lot of space when you aren't actually trying to garage your rig can get real small, particularly with others trying to get in and out of the facility at the same time. This might seem like a small thing, but we promise you a lot of headaches and flaring tempers will be avoided *if* you can get your rig in and out easily. This is particularly so if you aren't all that proficient at backing up your big trailer into that small stall.

Theft is always a problem around most commercial storage areas. Even though your rig is locked up and snug in its stall, we recommend that you cover your boat and remove all valuables before you leave. Marine electronic devices are particularly appealing for thieves, so don't leave any in your boat. Make sure that you have a good, solid padlock on the stall door.

Open Lot Storage

This commonly-used method is very popular in many parts of the country. It can be very convenient and much less expensive than covered stalls. When you keep your boat outside, however, it will be exposed to all sorts of weather, resulting in increased deterioration, plus the risk of pilferage and theft. So, as with keeping your boat in your driveway, we recommend you install a good-quality cover on your boat.

In addition to a boat cover, many boat owners use a lot

Figure 22. *Stacked Boat Storage.* This shows a storage facility immediately adjacent to a large reservoir in Texas. Boats stored here are lifted directly into the water by a specially modified, large forklift. After the day's fun on the water, the boats are returned to their slots in the structure.

of creativity in the construction of individual **boat shelters,** particularly in areas of our nation where there are severe winters. These shelters are designed to take the brunt of the ice and snow during the winter months.

Some boaters utilize a **shrink-wrap storage technique** that can be effective in keeping the elements, and you, out of the boat until spring, at a reasonable cost.

As open lots tend to be more vulnerable than other storage modes, theft and vandalism are a continual problem. We would accordingly recommend that you keep your boat only in an adequately secured, well-lit facility.

It is also important that your written storage agreement specify who's responsible for losses due to theft or vandalism while the boat is on the premises, as well as who pays for personal or property damages.

Off-the-Trailer Storage

Let's talk now about storing your boat off its trailer. Our previous comments about written storage agreements, theft and vandalism, boat covers, and insurance apply here as well. As you go through this, remember that with the boat "off-the-trailer," you also have to make arrangements for the storage of your boat trailer, preferably nearby.

Stacked Storage

This method is popular in some areas where there are a large number of boats owned by folks who use the nearby waters on a regular basis, and where the climate is not too severe. These multi-storied, frame-like storage buildings usually have no closed sides. This permits a forklift, or some other lifting means, to take the boats off their trailers at ground level, and lift them into their storage spots inside the structure and back down again. If the facility is near

Figure 23. *Moored Storage.* This is a typical mooring. Note the room between the boats so that each can weathervane without danger of colliding with its neighbors. As the weather is relatively mild in this area, boats stay in the water all year 'round.

the water, boats can be moved directly between their storage locations and the water. Rental fees may be relatively inexpensive as these are multi-story, high-density facilities. That, however, may be offset by other services provided, which may increase the total price.

The boat trailers are usually stored nearby at ground level to permit the stored boats to be put back onto them easily. Boaters then launch normally at a nearby ramp. In other cases, stored boats are taken directly to the launch location and placed in the water by the facility's forklift.

Very high winds, heavy snows, and cold weather may play havoc to boats stored in this manner, as well as to the structures themselves. As the boats are fully exposed to the weather, they must be adequately covered and winterized.

Security of the stored boats may also be a problem. But as most of these structures are located within well-fenced areas with employees in the vicinity, the threat is somewhat mitigated. It would still be wise, however, to remove all valuables from your stored boat.

Moored Storage

This mode is found in many marinas in mild climates, where severe winter freeze-ups don't occur. A number of **moorings** (a mooring is a permanent, individual anchorage to which a boat may be secured) are installed in a sheltered harbor and rented to clients.

Boats are made fast to these moorings by their bows. They weathervane around with the changing winds. Boats stored in this manner must usually be evacuated by owners during times of really adverse weather.

Moored boats are ready to be used without the launching and recovering hassles. Although this method is quite expensive, its popularity is due to the convenience.

It is usually necessary for the marina management

Figure 24. Dock Storage. This photograph shows part of a marina on a large inland lake in Texas. This is a floating facility, rising and falling with the level of the lake. In some years, the lake level will vary from a high of 45 feet above normal pool to 25 feet below. The docked boats rise and fall with the marina.

to provide shuttle boat service between the shore and the moored boats, unless boat owners have their own dinghies.

As the boats are in the water all the time, they are fully exposed to inclement weather topside, plus the underwater marine growths below the waterline. A well-fitted **boat cover** is very important to slow down deterioration due to sun and weather, and to a provide a level of theft protection. Boat trailers are usually stored near the marina, sometimes at extra expense.

In the event of major weather disturbances, most moored boats are either moved by their owners to a safe anchorage, or else taken out of the water to be stored at some safe, shoreside location.

Did you know that **in-water storage** is the best *structurally* for your boat? This is because a boat hull is primarily designed to be supported by water, and not by trailer bunks or rollers. However, please note that a boat stored on a properly set-up boat trailer is not damaged while out of the water, *if* proper care is provided.

Docked

This is usually the most expensive method of storing your boat, but also the most convenient. Boats are immediately available for use by owners without the launching and recovering hassle.

Partially **covered stalls** on a dock, usually located within a marina, are leased to clients. In some places these docks are floating, and in other locations they are fixed. Floating docks are found where there are major water-level fluctuations, such as inland reservoirs and impoundments, and coastal locations where tidal movements are significant.

Boats are tied up in these stalls, and are usually available for immediate use. The instant availability of the boats is one of the main reasons for the popularity of this storage method.

As in moored storage, the docked boat is exposed to the effects of weather and underwater growths. Properly covered and secured, however, your boat is not physically harmed, except by very large storms and the effects of underwater marine growths. In the event of really severe weather, docked boats are moved by their owners, and temporarily stored at some safe, shore-side location.

As most docks have direct shoreline access with little control of who comes and goes, vandalism and theft can be a major problem. Our experience has been that these criminal events usually occur when there are large numbers of people using the waters on which the marina is located, such as major holidays in the summer. So keep your valuables out of the boat if you want to keep them yours.

As with a moored boat, your trailer will be parked somewhere around the marina, many times at extra cost, or back home in your garage, or wherever.

Boat Covers

A quality boat cover can pay for itself in a short time. The use of a good cover will not only help avoid premature aging of the boat due to the elements, but also reduce the incidence of theft of pricey items from the boat by hiding them from persons passing by.

There are many kinds of boat covers on the market these days. These range from plastic, one-size-fits-all covers that flap in the slightest breeze, to the best quality, custom-made canvas models. There are essentially two types of **boat covers:** storage and travel.

A **storage cover,** made of canvas, or heavy duck,

works well and is very durable. We recommend that you do *not* use a plastic boat cover, or one made of any other non-porous material. A major problem with these is that moisture is trapped inside, increasing the corrosion problems on your boat.

Storage covers are used if you just want to protect your boat while in storage. Don't take one on the road, as it'll flap badly unless tied down like a mummy. Incidentally, we've used canvas storage covers with good results on boats stored both in the water and on land.

If you are on the road with your rig a lot, we recommend that you get a **travel cover.** These are made of tightly fitting canvas, and designed to withstand highway speeds. These, of course, can be used for storage purposes as well as for traveling. You get them from your boat dealer and by mail order. They are also available custom-tailored to your boat at local canvas shops.

Although the custom-tailored covers cost more than stock models, they can be a good investment in terms of thefts prevented, boat deterioration delayed, and the pleasure of having a cover that fits right.

The matter of fit can be important. One of life's lesser joys is putting about 300 square feet of badly fitting, flopping wet canvas on your boat on a cold, windy night.

More Comments on Theft

We strongly feel that the individual boat owner can contribute a lot to security by not storing valuables aboard a boat. This means fishing tackle, radios, electronic gear, tools, and any other easily removed, high-value item.

Now this is inconvenient without a doubt, but this type of property, left aboard, *will* be stolen. There is a threat anywhere you store your boat, but you can reduce it by removing tempting objects completely, and by securing other items on board in locked cabinets or storage areas.

Another thing you might do is to take a look at your boat from the standpoint of a thief. Knowing that *a thief's main enemies are noise, time, and light* can help you create a better defense of your property. The bad guys usually want to slip in and out under cover of darkness, quickly and silently, and pick up their loot with the least amount of fuss.

> *You should set things up so that it takes that bad guy a long, hard time to get to anything of value on your boat, he has to work in light, and he can't do it in silence.*

If you can create these conditions, your theft threat should be reduced. On-board noise and visual alarm systems are useful, but they must be carefully selected for the environment in which they will be used. We have found that a simple, pin-switch alarm system used on storage cabinets works well in fresh water. This is provided that actuating mechanisms and circuits are regularly lubricated with silicon spray, and their power supply is kept constant. Such systems are available at many auto parts stores.

These alarm systems are powered by the boat's electrical system. This means that the boat's battery must be recharged to compensate for the alarm's current consumption. Either a dockside recharger or operating the boat's engine(s) would take care of that. We haven't tried commercially available solar panels, but they should be suitable to recharge your boat's system.

We've found no alarm system that will withstand the corrosive effects of salt water or salt air for more than a few weeks.

It is wise to be aware of the liability limits of the

facility where you rent boat storage. The owners of these facilities usually assume no liability for losses or damages on their premises, hence the familiar "Not Responsible for Losses or Damages" signs.

Finally, as you consider the various storage options, contact the local law enforcement agencies. Ask what the recent incident rates have been for the facilities in question, and if they have any recommendations from a law enforcement standpoint. You may not like what you hear, but at the very least you will be informed before you sign that agreement.

> *If you don't know where you're going you will wind up somewhere else.*
>
> *Yogi Berra,* Wall Street Journal

NOTES

Chapter 7

Marine Insurance—Nothing Will Ever Happen to Me!

> *This chapter provides you with important information about insurance so you can decide what is best for your unique situation.*

Some Facts About Insurance

Please note that we are not providing legal advice or legal opinions here. See a qualified attorney for that. Having said that...

You may think that nothing will ever happen to you, but, unfortunately, accidents do happen. The proper insurance can do much to ease their financial impact.

Your insurance:

⚓ Should protect you from legal actions people take against you for bodily injury, and property damage you do to others

⚓ Should reimburse you for damages to your person, your passengers, and your property because of the actions of others, your own actions, and any other actions, including Acts of God

Your boat, its engine(s), equipment, and cargo are normally covered in a **marine insurance policy,** with the boat's trailer either in an endorsement to that policy, or covered separately by an auto insurance policy.

The cost of **marine insurance** is determined by various underwriting factors. These include the levels of coverage you want, the make and type of your boat, its hull material, the installed safety equipment, and the number and horsepower of the engine(s). How and where the boat will be used are considered, as well as your past boating experience, any training programs you've attended, the types and number of prior claims you've made, your automobile driving record, and your boat's top speed.

Incidentally, there may be a rate break at 40 MPH, so if your boat can go faster, you might pay a higher premium. It's like your swanky, new BMW costing a lot more to insure than an old work truck.

All of these factors, and more, enter into your insurability rating, and the annual premium you'll be paying. The **marine insurance carriers** get this information when you fill out their **Marine Insurance Application** forms. These detailed forms are also used as **"Requests for Quotation"** by some companies.

You must *accurately* and *truthfully* provide the information on these forms. Any inaccurate data you provide can operate to your great disadvantage. Many boaters have lived to regret those "little white lies" put on their applications in hopes of getting a lower rate.

We recommend that you deal with large, nationally-known insurance companies. The more **boat insurance** a company writes, the cheaper it gets. We also recommend that you deal with only those companies that have local representatives in the areas where you will be operating your rig. Dealing by mail, through an 800-number, or through voice mail can be an exercise in extreme frustration.

A good place to find an insurance company is in the Yellow Pages. Also ask other boaters who may have had experience with local representatives. Another good source of information is your boat dealer.

In seeking coverage, you should contact several insurance companies and submit application forms to each for a rate quotation. It really pays to shop around, as there can be a variance between the different companies.

If you aren't sure just what you want in the way of insurance coverage, advise the insurance agents and they will develop exclusive proposals just for you. Naturally, when you compare these proposals to make your decision, make sure you're comparing like offers.

Some insurance companies will write all the marine insurance they can for a time, and then stop if their losses become too high. This can be a real problem to a boater, because such companies may not choose to renew your policy. So, in making your decision, ask each company's representative to show you a sample marine insurance policy, and explain just what his company's policies are about losses, claims, *and* policy renewals.

Also, some insurance companies offer good boat policies, but may not insure your complete trailer boating rig without your having other insurance, such as auto, or home insurance, with them.

After you've received the proposals from several companies, *go over each one carefully.* Get help from an experienced friend, or some other party, if you feel the need. Your lawyer may need to be involved if you think you have complex requirements.

As insurance can be very confusing, it is essential that you find out from your insurance carriers all the details in their policies. You must know, for example, exactly how much, how, and to whom the **insurance carrier** will reimburse in the event of losses, and exactly how much the various coverages will cost you. Remember...

While the sweet words of the insurance salesman are always music to the ear, never forget that when it comes to paying claims, his company is guided entirely by the written terms of your policy.

So know exactly what coverage you are buying and what it really costs. Then you can logically evaluate its adequacies for your particular situation. *Read that fine print very carefully.*

You should know that there are generally two types of boat policies. The **Agreed Value Policy (AVP),** and the **Actual Cash Value Policy (ACV).**

The AVP specifies that the amount of insurance you have in force on your rig will be what you get in the event of a total loss. This value should be adjusted annually as the value of your insured items change with age.

IMPORTANT

The ACV policy is the most common. In the event of a total loss, you will receive the book value of the property involved. Yet each year when the coverage is renewed, you will pay the same rate as in previous years. This can lead you to think that your rig is insured for its original value, but it really isn't. You are insured only for the depreciated value of your property at the time of loss.

Once again, please do not rely solely on anyone's words on insurance coverage. See, in writing, exactly what you'll be getting. This seems like an obvious point, but so many otherwise street-smart folks ignore it. I guess the thought of reading all that fine print is just too much.

It's been rumored that some agents are so eager to sell boat insurance that they will actually lie to the companies they represent about your boat's top speed, your automobile driving record, or other key underwriting factors, to get your boat insured at lower rates.

You may think this low rate is a really good deal, and sign up and pay the premium. Then later the insurance carrier discovers that your boat really goes a lot faster than you stated, or that you do have automobile traffic violations on your record; or some other falsehood comes to light. This leads to swift cancellation of your policy. Now you are sitting on the beach with no insurance coverage, and your agent doesn't answer your calls.

So out you go to find some other boat insurance coverage. But now you've been "refused coverage," or "had coverage canceled," and you may be an "unacceptable risk." So you're stuck with a boat rig you shouldn't operate because of no insurance.

All this points out the fact that it is essential that boat owners be very careful who they deal with, and be completely honest with any statements made on any insurance document.

> *Never allow a sales agent, or anybody else, to talk you into putting any untrue statements on an insurance application with the promise that he can get you "a really good deal," or for any other reason.*

If anybody ever pitches that to you, it is strongly recommended that you have no further dealings with that person. Further, you should also consider reporting the person to the local Better Business Bureau, and/or your state's Board of Insurance.

We recommend also that you take videos or **photographs** of your boat, engine, and trailer, as well as the usual gear you keep aboard. These should be clear enough to show the condition of the items pictured. They should be dated, and kept in a secure place off the boat, preferably with your rig's ownership and insurance papers.

It is also a good idea to engrave, or otherwise permanently inscribe, each high-value item with your driver's license number or some other identifying mark.

Things to Find out from an Insurance Agent

In your dealings with insurance agents, there are some specific items to examine. When you discuss these, have the proposed insurance policy on the table in front of you.

Get a clear explanation of all the terms in the policy. For example, who exactly are the "covered persons"? What does "bodily injury," or "property damage," "equipment and accessories" really mean?

You need to know exactly where and when your policy applies. Is it "anywhere" or "anytime," or are there any geographical limitations or other exclusions? Is it good only during daylight hours in the summer when the sky is blue, and the birds are singing? Will you be covered when you're in some Mexican or Canadian fishing port, spending a boisterous night on the town?

You will probably want **"deductibles"** in your policy. Check what you can get and how they will be applied. Are they to be applied, once for payment to each occurrence of physical loss or damage, or is there some other schedule?

How about the **salvage charges** that come into play if you smash your own boat, or somebody else's, beyond repair? Will your insurance company pay for raising, protecting, removing, and/or destroying the damaged vessels?

How about **towing services** to get you back home when you break down while on the water? Are there any limitations on payments to be made to you for this service? This can be an important consideration if you operate on big water.

Will a new boat you buy during the term of your policy be covered like that really cool, 24-foot Gutwrencher deep-V with the twin 200 HP BelchFire engines you fell for at the boat show? Do you have coverage if that new rig replaces your old 14-foot scow? Are both covered if you decide to keep the scow and the Gutwrencher?

What are your duties under the policy when losses or damages occur? Is there a time limit for reporting losses? Do you have to show the insurance company any of the damaged property? If so, where and how do you report the losses or damages? Is a telephone report OK, or does it have to be in writing? Is police or sheriff verification required?

If there is injury or property damage to someone else arising from your or your boat's actions, or lack of action, will your insurance company defend you in court? Will they pay for damages for which you and any other covered person are found legally liable? When will they pay?

If you operate your boat in excess of a marina's "no-wake" speed limit, and your wake causes a person to be thrown overboard from a moored boat, with resulting injuries, will your insurance policy cover you for litigated damages?

Will your insurance company pay the necessary medical and/or funeral expenses resulting from injury to anyone while in, on, boarding, departing, or being towed by your boat? How long after the date of the injury will such expenses be covered?

Are you covered by the provisions of your insurance policy if you operate someone else's boat and cause damage to that boat? Or what if you smash into a pier and damage the pier, or a passenger aboard the boat gets hurt? Or what if somebody else's boat causes damage to that boat while you are both underway?

Will the insurance company pay medical and/or funeral expenses for a trespasser if he is injured or killed while stealing gear from your boat?

Is there coverage to your boat or engine for freezing or ice damage, for mechanical breakdowns, for damage due to striking an underwater obstruction, or for the repair of defective parts?

How about coverage for bodily injury or property damage claims involving your boat trailer?

Is there any duplication of coverage with your automobile insurance?

Are the actions you must take when someone is injured or damage is incurred clearly spelled out in the policy? How about those actions you *don't take,* sometimes called "omissions?"

Would your insurance company defend you if legal action were taken against you, for, say, failing to render aid to a disabled boat while underway, if by doing so you thought you would place your own boat at risk?

If there is a **"passenger for hire"** proviso in the insurance contract, you should be cautious. There have been successful litigations in the past involving injuries against boat owners because these boat owners accepted contributions to the boat's operating expenses from guests or crew. This was modified in the Passenger Vessel Safety Act of 1993, but you should be aware that if you make the provision of any item a "condition for carriage" on your boat, you now have a "passenger for hire" situation.

These questions should stimulate your thinking. Get the answers to these, and any others you will certainly have, from the insurance companies you are considering for coverage.

Make sure you have your insurance coverage clearly thought through, and fully priced, before you close on any boat purchase.

Too many well-meaning folks get into more hassles over insurance than you can imagine. If you purchase your boat from a boat dealer, the matter of insurance is usually discussed. If it isn't, bring it up.

If you decide to buy your boat rig from a private party, you're on your own. You must be extremely careful about using another person's boating rig without there being in place adequate marine and trailer insurance that covers you. Those "famous last word" quotes should include a boat seller's saying to a buyer, "No sweat, you take my boat to the lake; I'm too busy right now. Really try her out, my insurance covers you just fine." This is the kind of situation that makes lawyers grin and nudge each other as they think about maybe putting a new BMW in their driveway.

> *When praying does no good insurance does help.*
>
> Bertolt Brecht, "The Mother"

NOTES

Appendix

Basic Marine Terms

Please note that the nautical terms in this Appendix are just the tip of the iceberg. What you get here are the common expressions used by recreational power boaters around marinas, docks, launch ramps, and almost anywhere else we gather. Blue-water sea talk, virtually another language, is not translated here!

Boat Terms

Visualize standing in the middle of your boat facing forward. You are looking at the boat's **bow,** the boat's forwardmost part. If you are at the widest point of the boat, you are at its **beam.**

Still facing forward, gaze left and you are looking to **port.** Now gaze right and you are seeing the **starboard** side. Look to the rear, **aft,** and you will see the **stern,** the boat's back end. That's where the boat's **transom,** or **stern panel,** is located.

In the middle of your boat, you are **amidships** and are probably near your boat's **helm,** the steering station. You are in the boat's **cockpit,** and standing on the **deck,** also called the **sole.**

While at the helm, note the boat's navigational instruments. It may be equipped with a **Magnetic Compass, LORAN-C,** and/or **Global Positioning System (GPS).**

Ease over to either the port or starboard side. When you get there, you'll be at the **gunwale** (pronounced "gun'l"). This is the top edge of the boat's side.

Look down over the gunwale and you should see the **rubrail,** a rope, plastic, or metal protective molding that goes around both sides of the hull from bow to stern on many boats.

Look over the side and you see the boat's **waterline.** This is the line around the hull to which the boat is immersed while at rest.

Keep looking down and note the boat's **freeboard,** the vertical distance between the waterline and the deck.

Most small power boats, except for the very small and bare-bones models, are equipped by their manufacturer with **running lights** (navigation lights) as approved by the U.S. Coast Guard. It is very important that your boat be properly illuminated if you operate at any time after dark, or in reduced visibility.

The boat's **Personal Flotation Devices (PFDs),** also called "life jackets" or "life preservers," or "Mae Wests," should be at-hand in, or near, the cockpit.

If your boat is outfitted for fishing, it probably has one or more **live wells.** These are small tanks, usually with an aerator, where live bait and your catch may be kept.

You might also see one or more **downriggers** on that fishing boat. These devices, which look like miniature cranes mounted on the stern and/or gunwales, take your fishing lures down to where the big fish swim. When Old Lunker strikes the lure, your line is pulled free from the downrigger's line. This enables the fish to be fought and landed without the encumbrance of the heavy lead weights needed to get that lure way down.

If your boat is so equipped, it will have a **head,** the commode, and maybe even a **galley,** the on-board kitchen.

When you get the boat moving, you are **underway.** A boat's motion forward through the water is called the **headway.** A fast enough speed to enable the boat to readily respond to her helm is called **steerageway.**

If you are moving in the same direction as the wind, you are said to be going **downwind, or before the wind.**

If your boat **broaches,** she turns sideways to the wind. If the wind and waves are strong enough, the boat may **swamp,** that is, take on large quantities of water over her sides. This is a dangerous situation, and our smart Skipper will now try to get her **bailed out,** and try to get **in the lee** of something, which is shelter behind an island or peninsula, out of the wind.

The **lee shore** is the direction **to which** the wind is going. The **windward** shore is in the direction **from which** the wind is blowing.

If the engine quits en route, our Skipper may decide to deploy his **sea anchor,** a canvas or plastic truncated cone with a bridle on the large end. Fastened to the bow cleat, or bow eye, it keeps the boat pointed into the wind while the boat drifts **downwind.**

If the boat is in possible danger of crashing into a rocky shore, the Skipper may decide to deploy his **ground tackle** (the **anchor,** its **chain, shackles,** and **rode**—the anchor line), and ride out the blow while **standing off** from that shore at anchor.

If the Skipper ever feels that there is a life-threatening situation, he will call the local Coast Guard for help on the boat's **VHF radio,** saying **MAYDAY, MAYDAY, MAYDAY.**

But now the wind dies down, the seas flatten. Skipper gets the engine fired up again. He decides to **steer a course** for the nearest harbor to get his balky **inboard engine** fixed. So he **weighs anchor** (lifts it and departs).

Using **dead reckoning** (a method of navigation based on the formula, Distance = Rate × Time) our stalwart Skipper heads for that harbor.

He makes his **ETA** (Estimated Time of Arrival), moves past the **jetties** (long, narrow rock piles coming out from the shore to protect the harbor entrance), and moves into the harbor.

He comes to a floating buoy with large letters saying, **NO-WAKE ZONE.** Being an Old Salt, he cuts his speed to less than 5 MPH so his vessel won't produce any discernible wake.

Now he heads for the **fuel stall** to refill his tanks and inquire about maintenance service on that engine. Fueling done, he pulls out of the fuel stall and **docks** in the nearby **transient stall** to await arrival of the maintenance folks.

Some Flotsam and Jetsam?

Flotsam meant everything floating on the surface after a vessel had sunk. **Jetsam** was the stuff thrown overboard during a heavy storm to help save a vessel. These terms have evolved over the years, and now, in addition to their original meanings, are used in reference to anything washed up on a beach, tossed around by the waves, or the interesting material in this section.

"Starboard" is a modern derivation of the old "steering board" used on very early sailing ships. The steering board on an ancient ship was located on the right-hand side, looking forward toward the bow. The left-hand side is called the **"port"** side. The ancient vessels always tied up to a dock with their steering boards on the outside to facilitate control after casting off. The other side, being next to the dock, thus became known as the "port" side.

The commonly used word **"posh"** came out of a nautical heritage. Many years ago, ships used to regularly sail from England, around Gibraltar, thence west on the Mediterranean Sea, through the Suez Canal, and onward to India, then an important part of the British Empire.

This was before the days of air conditioning, and it got

mighty hot on those ships in the summer months. It was wise to book a cabin out of the direct sunshine as much as possible. It proved best to have a cabin on the port side outbound from England, and on the starboard side on the way back home. So the gentry would book their passage with the notation "Port Outbound Starboard Home" in their letter requests for passage. This expression evolved into "P.O.S.H.," which in turn became "posh," meaning "ritzy," or "snazzy" today.

Here's another, less pleasant tale. Among **blue-water** (open ocean) sailors in the early years, there was the belief that all sailing ships had souls. New vessels got their souls from young maidens strapped alive just under the **bow-sprit** (a short spar on the bow of sailing ships) on the ship's first, or "maiden" voyage.

When these young ladies died, their souls passed to their ships, to remain until the ships sank or were otherwise lost. The souls then were free to leave for the Great Beyond. These human sacrifices were to appease Neptune, the great god of the sea, and Davy Jones, the sailor's devil. "Davy Jones' Locker" means the bottom of the ocean, the grave of all those who perish at sea.

As civilization advanced, the use of live maidens mercifully stopped, to be replaced by beautifully carved figureheads. These figureheads to this day are always of human beings, usually female, and never animals or fish.

More modern definitions include:

"A **boat** is hole in the water where you throw money."

"A **boater** is only truly happy on two days—the day he buys his boat, and the day he sells it."

Trailer Terms

The **coupler** is on the end of the trailer tongue. It connects the trailer to the tow vehicle. Inside the coupler is the **ball**

clamp, which grabs the base of the **ball hitch** on the tow vehicle.

The **trunk connector end** of the trailer's **wishbone wiring harness** is usually routed through the trailer's **tongue,** to the tow vehicle's electrical system.

The **safety chains** are attached to the trailer's tongue right behind the coupler. They are hooked to the tow vehicle when the rig is on the road.

The **bow post** is located behind the coupler on the trailer's tongue. Its purpose is to hold the bow of the boat with the **bow stop,** and, in some designs, to provide a platform to support the **winch.**

The **winch** is used to pull the boat onto the trailer when **recovering** (returning the boat to its trailer after it has been **launched**). The winch can be hand-operated, or maybe electrically powered, if the boat weighs more than about 2000 pounds.

The **bow hold down,** either nylon strapping, cable, light chain, or line, prevents the boat from thrusting forward over the bow post into the back of the tow vehicle in the event of a front-end collision. We can tell you from long experience that this simple item can be a lifesaver.

The trailer's main frame bears the load of the boat from the **boat supports.** These are either hard plastic, or hard rubber rollers, padded wood members, or some combination of both, called **"stringers"** or **"bunks."** The boat rides on top, and is supported by, these members.

Certain trailer designs feature a **hinged frame** to enable tilting of the trailer. This gives much easier launching and recovering of larger boats.

The tow vehicle's electrical power, as routed through the trailer's **electrical system,** operates the trailer's power winch (although in some configurations the winch is on a separate circuit), and the tail, brake, turn signal, license plate, and running lights.

The **boat tie downs** are another important trailer component. One commonly used tie down employs a nylon strap across the boat, about a third of the way forward from the stern, secured on both sides of the trailer's frame. Another method is a pair of nylon straps secured on the transom to the water-ski tow cycs, and then on down the trailer's frame.

Organizations Involved in Boating

As you get involved in power boating, you will be amazed at the popularity of the sport. In fact, over 30 percent of all Americans participate in some way or another. There are many public, and thousands of private, organizations whose entire concern is recreational boating. Those that we show here are the most useful, as the services they perform directly influence every power boater.

The Federal Government

In the course of your boating experiences, you will probably have many contacts with your Federal government. Usually your contacts will be pleasant, helpful, and in some cases, positively uplifting, like when that Coast Guardsman hauls you out of the water.

Three Federal agencies house the folks you will most often deal with in your boating adventures.

United States Coast Guard (USCG)

The USCG is one of the oldest of our Federal agencies, dating back to the 1700s. It is a military service, which in peacetime is part of the Department of Transportation. In times of conflict it becomes, either wholly or partially, part

Commandant
U.S. Coast Guard Headquarters
Washington, DC 20593-0001
Toll free telephone: (800) 336-2628

Coast Guard District Offices

FIRST DISTRICT
408 Atlantic Avenue
Boston, MA 02210
(617) 223-8310
All New England to Toms River,
New Jersey, and parts of New York.

SECOND DISTRICT
1430 Olive Street
St. Louis, MO 63103
(314) 425-5971
Mississippi River System (except
south of Baton Rouge) and the Illinois River north of Joliet.

FIFTH DISTRICT
431 Crawford Street
Portsmouth, VA 23704
(804) 398-9505
Maryland, Delaware, Washington,
DC, Virginia, North Carolina, and
parts of New Jersey, Pennsylvania

SEVENTH DISTRICT
909 SE 1st Avenue
Miami, FL 33131
(305) 536-5698
South Carolina, Georgia, amd most
of Florida and Puerto Rico and adjacent U.S. Islands.

EIGHTH DISTRICT
500 Camp Street
New Orleans, LA 70130
(504) 589-2972
Western Florida, parts of Alabama,
Mississippi, and Louisiana, Texas
and New Mexico

NINTH DISTRICT
1240 East 9th Street
Cleveland, OH 44199
(216) 522-4422
Michigan, parts of Ohio, Illinois,
Indiana, Minnesota, Wisconsin,
New York, and Pennsylvania.

ELEVENTH DISTRICT
400 Oceangate
Long Beach, CA 90822
(213) 499-5310
California, Arizona, Nevada, and
Utah.

THIRTEENTH DISTRICT
915 Second Avenue
Seattle, WA 98174
(206) 442-7355
Oregon, Washington, Idaho, and
Montana.

TENTH DISTRICT
300 Ala Moana Boulevard
Honolulu, HI 96850
(808) 546-7130/546-7109
Hawaii, and certain Pacific Islands.

SEVENTEENTH DISTRICT
P.O. Box 3-5000
Juneau, AK 99802
(907) 586-7467
Alaska

of the Department of Defense, serving under United States Navy jurisdiction.

The USCG's regular activities include setting and enforcing vessel safety standards; monitoring and enforcing pollution control matters; providing certain ice-breaking services, enforcing off-shore fishing regulations to 200 miles; and interdicting illegal alien and drug movements.

In addition, the USCG operates thousands of Navigational Aids, including radio beacons and LORAN-C installations; rescues persons in distress; and is deeply involved in all aspects of marine safety. The state Boat Registration System, now well established, stemmed from Federal legislation in 1971, promulgated by the USCG.

The policies and regulations formulated at Coast Guard Headquarters are enforced or carried out locally on a face-to-face basis with the public in the Coast Guard Districts shown below. The various District Commanders have personnel, ships, and airplanes under their control for this purpose.

With USCG Headquarters housed in Washington, D.C., the operational functions are exercised through 10 subordinate districts. There are eight districts in the Continental United States (CONUS), with districts in Alaska and Hawaii.

The following provides you with a handy information source wherever you may be in the United States. If you have any questions about the technical and practical aspects of power boating, give these folks a ring for help.

In the matrix on the following page, the geographical areas served by each district follow each entry. You will also note that the districts are not consecutively numbered.

U.S. Coast Guard Auxiliary

In 1939, the U.S. Coast Guard Auxiliary was created to assist the U.S. Coast Guard in promoting safety on the water. The Auxiliary is a volunteer, non-military organization maintaining close affiliation with the USCG. It is the only boating organization so authorized and has more than 1,200 "flotillas" throughout all 50 States, Puerto Rico, the Virgin Islands, American Samoa, and Guam. Its membership exceeds 40,000 men and women.

Persons wishing to join the Auxiliary are encouraged to contact the nearest Coast Guard or Auxiliary unit, or to call the **Boating Safety Hotline** at **1-800-368-5647** for additional information.

Although the Auxiliary participates in a wide variety of activities, its three basic programs are **Public Education, Operational Missions,** and **Courtesy Marine Examinations (CME).**

Public Education courses are designed to meet the needs of particular segments of the boating community.

The Boating Skills and Seamanship Program is a six-lesson core course, with seven additional optional lessons selected according to local needs and interests.

The Sailing and Seamanship Course parallels the Boating Skills course for those interested in sailboating.

The Advanced Coastal Navigation Course is a 12-lesson program for persons who have completed either one of the above courses.

In addition to these three regular courses, the Auxiliary presents a special short lecture program in boating safety for schools, churches, and other organizations.

All of the above courses and programs are tuition-free, with the only cost being nominal charges for course materials.

The Auxiliary's **Operational Missions** help thousands of recreational boaters who find themselves in trouble on the water. Auxiliarists cooperate with state boating officials and the USCG to augment their forces for search and rescue missions, safety patrols, and regatta patrols.

In many cases unseen, these highly qualified boatmen are a major force in improving safety on our waterways.

The **Courtesy Marine Examination (CME)** program is another basic activity of the Auxiliary. These safety checks are provided as a free public service, performed at the request of the boat owner or operator. The examiners performing this service are all Auxiliary members who have been carefully trained to look for some of the more common problems which might occur in your boat or its related safety equipment.

We highly recommend that all boaters take advantage of this program wherever possible. The price is right, and the discussions with the CME folks can be useful.

Skippers are advised to call the Boating Safety Hotline toll-free at 1-800-368-5647, or their local Auxiliary unit, to obtain additional CME information.

Federal Communications Commission (FCC)

The FCC is responsible for an extremely wide range of domestic communication activities. It regulates interstate and foreign radio and wire communications; prescribes qualifications and classifications for operators; issues operator and station licenses; and manages many and varied frequencies allocated to private, commercial, and government users in the United States. Their address is: Federal Communications Commission, Aviation & Marine Division, 2025 M Street NW, Washington, DC 20554; (202) 632-7197.

Don't let that high-sounding name "Ship Station" lead you to think that the $25, used VHF radio you hooked up in the old johnboat isn't included here, because it is.

You *don't need* a Radio Operator's Permit to use your VHF radio (or other telecommunicating equipment) in the

United States. However, if you plan to dock at a foreign port, you must have the Restricted Radiotelephone Operator Permit (RP). Call the FCC to get the Form 753 to apply for your RP.

You *do need* a "Ship Radio Station License" for the VHF radio, and for EPIRB, Radar, Single Side Band radios, plus some other telecommunication equipment. Note that this license is not required for using a Citizens Band (CB) radio on your boat.

You get this Ship Radio Station License by applying to the FCC Private Radio Bureau Licensing Division, Box 1040, Gettysburg, PA 17325; (717) 337-1212 on FCC Form 506. These forms come along with some new radios, but if you can't find one, ask the FCC at a local office (check the telephone book), or at the preceding address, to get one. You will note that your Ship Radio Station License is issued to *both* you and your boat.

When the FCC sends you that new station license, it must be posted aboard the vessel named thereon. If you move the licensed radio to another vessel, the FCC must be advised, and the Ship Radio Station License modified. If you sell the boat with the radio, the license must be modified. Contact the FCC for the details regarding these changes.

There are a couple of items that should be mentioned about using the VHF radio.

⚓ Before you depress your "transmit" button, make sure nobody is talking on your channel. When you do talk, make it short and clear.

⚓ Except for the Marine Telephone Operator channels 25, 26, and 28, conversations on all other channels must be held to the absolute minimum.

⚓ It is important that Channel 16, as the **hailing channel,** be kept free of chatter at all times. This means all parties shift immediately to either Channel 68, 69, 71, 72, or 78 after making initial contact on Channel 16.

Your VHF radio is an important safety device aboard your boat. As such, all transmissions on any channel, except the marine telephone channels, must be of an operational or safety nature.

The range of your VHF transmission is around 20 miles if you have a 25-watt radio with an 8-foot antenna. The hand-held 5-watt radios have a range of about a mile. They are primarily useful around ports and harbors, and close-range communications between vessels. They should not be considered your primary VHF capability.

Be advised that the Feds, and many other folks with law enforcement badges, take a dim view of the improper use of VHF.

The use of obscene, indecent, or profane language during radio communications is punishable by a $10,000 fine, imprisonment for two years, or both. Be aware that your VHF transmissions are monitored on a random and regular basis by the FCC, the Coast Guard, and several other Federal and state agencies.

The National Weather Service (NWS)

This Federal agency prepares the weather forecasts and reports as regularly seen in the various media. The NWS is a part of the National Oceanic and Atmospheric Administration (NOAA), which belongs to the United States Department of Commerce. The NWS headquarters is located at 8060 13th Street, Silver Spring, MD 20910; (301) 443-8910.

As Skipper, you need to know as accurately as possible what weather conditions will be encountered during any contemplated voyage. This information can be obtained from several sources, depending on what sort of boating you have in mind.

The best source for detailed marine information is the National Weather Service/NOAA's continuous weather broadcasts. These round-the-clock broadcasts can be heard on the marine VHF radio in your boat, and/or on those little battery-powered, weather-only radios. These receive only the two frequencies that NWS utilizes in your geographic area. This means there is no fiddling around with a dial when you want to get the weather. Just turn the thing on to whichever of the two frequencies sounds the best.

In addition to the NWS, the larger Coast Guard stations also broadcast regularly scheduled weather information.

As mentioned earlier, commercial radio and TV stations usually broadcast weather information on locally available schedules. But whatever the broadcast media, the NWS is the governmental agency that provides the actual meteorological information. This data is obtained from a wide variety of sources all over the world, and in the case of the weather satellites, out of this world.

State Boating Offices

You must register your boat in the state where it will be principally used. A **"Certificate of Numbers"** will be issued upon registration, and this number must be displayed on your boat. Check with your State Boating Office regarding numbering procedures, and other requirements for boating in your state.

You must notify the State Boating Office which issued your **Certificate of Numbers** within 15 days if:

⚓ Your boat is transferred, destroyed, abandoned, lost, stolen, or recovered; or,

⚓ Your certificate of number is lost, destroyed, or the owner's address changes,

Included here are all the State Boating Offices in the United States. Contact the office in your state if there are any questions pertaining to safety or state regulations covering the operation of your vessel.

ALABAMA
Marine Police Division
Department of Conservation
Folsom Building
Montgomery, AL 36130
(205) 261-3673

ALASKA
Department of Natural Resources
P.O. Box 3-5000
Juneau, AK 99802-1217
(907) 586-7467

ARIZONA
Game & Fish Department
2222 West Greenway Road
Phoenix, AZ 85023
(602) 942-3000

ARKANSAS
Boating Safety Section
No. 2 Natl. Resources Dr.
Little Rock, AR 72205
(501) 223-6377

CALIFORNIA
Department of Boating & Waterways
1629 S Street
Sacramento, CA 95814
(916) 445-6281

COLORADO
Division of Parks
13787 South Highway 85
Littleton, CO 80125
(313) 791-1957

CONNECTICUT
Office of Boating Safety
P.O. Box 280
Old Lyme, CT 06371
(203) 434-8638

DELAWARE
Fish & Wildlife Division
P.O. Box 1401
Dover, DE 19903
(302) 736-3440

FLORIDA
Department of Natural Resources
3900 Commonwealth Blvd.
Tallahassee, FL 32399
(904) 487-3671

GEORGIA
Department of Natural Resources
205 Butler Street, SE
East Tower, Suite 1366
Atlanta, GA 30334
(404) 656-3534

HAWAII
Department of Transportation
79 South Nimitz Highway
Honolulu, HI 96813
(808) 548-2515/548-2838

IDAHO
Department of Parks
Statehouse Mail
Boise, ID 83720
(208) 334-2284

ILLINOIS
Department of Conservation
524 South Second Street
Springfield, IL 62701
(217) 782-6431

INDIANA
Department of Natural Resources
606 State Office Building
Indianapolis, IN 46204
(317) 232-4010

IOWA
State Conservation Commission
Wallace Building
Des Moines, IA 50319
(515) 281-5919

KANSAS
Kansas Department of Parks
Route 2, Box 54A
Pratt, KS 67124
(316) 672-5911, ext. 108

KENTUCKY
Department of Natural Resources
Kentucky Water Patrol
107 Mero Street
Frankfort, KY 40601
(502) 564-3074

LOUISIANA
Department of Wildlife
P.O. Box 15570
Baton Rouge, LA 70895
(504) 765-2988

MAINE
Department of Wildlife
284 State St., Station 41
Augusta, ME 04333
(207) 289-2043

MARYLAND
Department of Natural Resources
Tawes State Office Building
Annapolis, MD 21401
(301) 974-2240

MASSACHUSETTS
Law Enforcement Division
100 Cambridge Street
Boston, MA 02202
(617) 727-1614

MICHIGAN
Department of Natural Resources
Steven T. Mason Building
P.O. Box 30028
Lansing, MI 48909
(517) 373-1650/373-1230

MINNESOTA
Boat & Water Safety
Box 46, 500 Lafayette Road
St. Paul, MN 55155-4046
(612) 296-3310

MISSISSIPPI
Wildlife Conservation
P.O. Box 451
Jackson, MS 39205
(601) 961-5300

MISSOURI
Department of Public Safety
P.O. Box 603
Jefferson City, MO 65102
(314) 751-3333

MONTANA
Boating Safety Division
1420 East 6th Street
Helena, MT 59620
(406) 444-4046

NEBRASKA
Game & Parks Commission
2200 North 33rd Street
P.O. Box 30370
Lincoln, NE 68503
(402) 464-0641

NEVADA
Nevada Department of Wildlife
P.O. Box 10678
Reno, NV 89520
(702) 789-0500

NEW JERSEY
Marine Law Enforcement
Box 7068
West Trenton, NJ 08628
(609) 882-2000, ext. 2530

NEW YORK
Marine & Recreational Vehicles
Agency Building No. 1
Empire State Plaza
Albany, NY 12238
(518)474-0445

NEW HAMPSHIRE
Marine Patrol
Hazen Drive
Concord, NH 03305
(603) 271-3336

NEW MEXICO
Boating Safety Section
P.O. Box 1147
Santa Fe, NM 87504-1147
(505) 827-3986

NORTH CAROLINA
Wildlife Resources Commission
Archdale Building
Raleigh, NC 27611
(919) 733-7191

NORTH DAKOTA
ND Game & Fish Department
100 N Bismarck Expressway
Bismarck, ND 58501-5095
(701) 221-6300

OHIO
Division of Watercraft
Fountain Square
Columbus, OH 43224
(614) 265-6480

OKLAHOMA
Department of Public Safety
P.O. Box 11415
Oklahoma City, OK 73136
(405) 424-4011, ext. 2143

OREGON
State Marine Board
3000 Market St., NE #505
Salem, OR 97310
(503) 378-8501

PENNSYLVANIA
Fish Commission
P.O. Box 1673
Harrisburg, PA 17105-1673
(717) 657-4538

PUERTO RICO
Department of Natural Resources
Commission of Navigation
P.O. Box 5887
Puerta de Tierra, PR 00906
(809) 724-2340

RHODE ISLAND
Boat Registration Office
22 Hayes Street
Providence, RI 02908
(401) 277-6647

SOUTH CAROLINA
Division of Boating
P.O. Box 12559
Charleston, SC 29412
(803) 795-6350

SOUTH DAKOTA
Department of Fish & Parks
Anderson Building
445 E Capitol
Pierre, SD 57501
(605) 773-3630

TENNESSEE
Wildlife Resources Agency
P.O. Box 40747
Nashville, TN 37204
(615) 360-0500

TEXAS
Parks and Wildlife Department
4200 Smith School Road
Austin, TX 78744
(512) 389-4850

U.S. VIRGIN ISLANDS
Department of Planning
179 Altona & Welgunst
Charlotte Amalie
St. Thomas, VI 00802
(809) 774-3320

UTAH
Division of Parks
1636 West Temple Street
Salt Lake City, UT 84116
(801) 533-4490

VERMONT
Marine Division
103 S Main St., Room 221
Waterbury, VT 05676
(802) 244-8778

VIRGINIA
Commission of Game
P.O. Box 11104
Richmond, VA 23230-1104
(804) 367-1000

WASHINGTON, DC
Harbor Patrol
550 Water Street, SW
Washington, DC 20024
(202) 727-4582

WASHINGTON
Parks & Recreation Commission
7150 Cleanwater Lane
Olympia, WA 98504
(206) 586-2165

WEST VIRGINIA
Law Enforcement Division
Department of Natural Resources
1800 Washington Street, E
Charleston, WV 25305

WISCONSIN
Bureau of Law Enforcement
P.O. Box 7921
Madison, WI 53707
(608) 266-2141

WYOMING
Game & Fish Department
5400 Bishop Boulevard
Cheyenne, WY 82002
(307) 777-7605

Other Boating Organizations

These organizations serve a wide variety of functions for recreational boaters. Use the addresses and telephone numbers to obtain the publications shown, or to receive more information.

American Boat and Yacht Council
P.O. Box 747
405 Headquarters Drive, Suite 3
Millersville, MD 21108
(301) 923-3932)

Develops and publishes "Standards and Recommended Practices for Small Craft" on designing, building, equipping, and maintaining pleasure and commercial watercraft. Also publishes "Boating Information: A Bibliography and Source List" which lists over 1,300 books, video, and other boating materials.

American Power Boat Association
17640 East Nine Mile Road
East Detroit, MI 48021
(313) 773-9700

National member organization and sanctioning body for power boat events and professional racing in the United States. Monthly publication is *Propeller.*

National HQ, American Red Cross
17th & D Streets, NW
Washington, DC 20006
(202) 639-3886

Sponsors basic boating, rescue, swimming, and water safety course. Publishes "Safe Boating" and "Safe Boating: A Parents' Guide." Contact your local chapter for additional information.

American Water Ski Association
P.O. Box 191
Winter Haven, FL 33880
(813) 324-4341

Organizing, sanctioning, and governing body for competitive U.S. water skiing. Publishes *Water Skier* magazine and instructional booklets on safety and water recreation.

Boat Owners Association of the U.S.
880 South Pickett Street
Alexandria, VA 22304
(703) 823-9550

A national, politically active, membership organization. Provides a wide variety of services, including a Consumer Protection Bureau, to help solve problems between boaters and the marine industry. Publishes the authoritative news-journal *BOATS / US Reports*. Many excellent member services, including boat financing, insurance, merchandise sales, towing insurance, and much more.

U.S. Foundation for Boating Safety
880 South Pickett Street
Alexandria, VA 22304
(703) 823-9550

National, non-profit boating safety organization. Researches safety issues and boating accidents; promotes boating education; produces and distributes free safety literature; maintains national boating reference library. 1-800-336-BOAT (in VA call 1-800-245-BOAT)

National HQ, U.S. Power Squadrons
1504 Blue Ridge Road
Box 30423
Raleigh, NC 27622

Private, non-profit national member organization of boating enthusiasts. Over 500 local squadrons offer public boating courses. For USPS boating course information please call (919) 821-0281.

Bibliography

Auerbach, Paul, *Medicine for the Outdoors*
(Boston, MA: Little Brown, 1991)

BOAT/U.S. Foundation For Boating Safety, *Boater's Source Directory*
(Arlington, VA: Boat/U.S., 1993)

Brotherton, Miner, *The 12 Volt Bible for Boats*
(Camden, ME: Seven Seas Press, 1985)

Buchanan, George, *The Boat Repair Manual*
(New York, NY: Arco Publications, 1985)

Carpenter, William, *Trailer Boater's Basic Handbook*
(San Antonio, TX: Gemini Marine, 1993)

Caswell, Christopher, *The Illustrated Book of Basic Boating*
(New York, NY: Hearst Marine Books, 1990)

Collins, Mike, *Fitting out a Fiberglass Hull*
(Dobbs Ferry, NY: Sheridan House, 1991)

Maloney, Elbert, *Chapman Piloting—Seamanship & Small
Boat Handling*
(New York, NY: Hearst Marine Books, 1987)

National Marine Manufacturers Association, *You and Your Trailer*
(Chicago, IL: NMMA, 1991)

Nicolson, Ian, *Boat Data Book*
(Dobbs Ferry, NY: Sheridan House, 1986)

Schneider, G., *How to Buy, Own, and Sell a Boat*
(Camden, ME: International Marine Publishing Company, 1990)

U.S. Coast Guard, *Requirements for Recreational Boats*
(Washington, DC: U.S. Government Printing Office)

U.S. Coast Guard, *Alcohol and Boating—Consumer Fact Sheet*
(Washington, DC: U.S. Government Printing Office, 1990)

Vigor, John, *The Practical Mariner's Book of Knowledge*
(Camden, ME: International Marine, 1994)

White, Peter, *Powerboating: A Guide to Sportsboat Handling*
(Brighton, England: Fernhurst Books, 1991)

YMCA of the USA, *Teaching Boating Safety*
(Champaign, IL: Human Kinetics Publishers, 1989)

Zadig, Ernest, *The Complete Book of Boating Knowledge*
(Englewood Cliffs, NJ: Prentice-Hall, 1984)

Other Great Publications

~~~~~~

BOAT/U.S. Reports, by the Boat Owners' Association of the United States. This glossy paper, bi-monthly, tabloid-size publication is an excellent publication for the recreational boater. It presents the status of the many legislative actions that directly involve the pleasure boater, as well as a Reader's Forum and excellent educational sections. We recommend you join BOAT/U.S. Call them at (703) 461-2866 for additional information.

BOAT/U.S. Annual Equipment Catalog is essentially a publication designed for selling boating items and services, but, in addition, lots of really good information is tucked into the nearly 400 pages. We have found this catalog most useful in keeping up with what's new in the marine marketplace, as well the many included tips and boating techniques. As a member of BOAT/U.S. you will receive this catalog free each year.

Coast Guard Consumer Fact Sheets, by the United States Coast Guard. These relatively short (2-3 pages) publications are issued periodically. They cover a range of timely items of great interest to recreational boaters. We recommend you contact the USCG at the Boating Hotline, 1-800-368-5647 (in the Washington, D.C. area call (202) 267-0780) to obtain the complete set or individual fact sheets.

Powerboat Reports, by Belvoir Publications. These are monthly reports of 30 or so pages filled with useful product reviews and evaluations of the many items used by recreational power boaters. This publication accepts no advertising. The product evaluations are accordingly unbiased. It is useful if you are in the market for an item for your boat. For further information, or to subscribe, call 1-800-829-9086.

NOTES

Index

C

D

G

I

J

K

L

large mirrors   100
lateral marks   158
Lateral System of Buoyage   158-159
launch ramp angst   97
lee shore   146
lee side   145
leeward   145
liens   46
limited-slip rear axle   99
live well   22
load limits   22
loan   39, 61
Local Notice to Mariners   76
LOng RAnge Navigation (LORAN)   81-82
lower unit   50, 107, 130, 187, 191

M

maintenance service records   45
make-ready   17, 40, 58
mandatory voyage termination   121
marine batteries   23
marine growths   185, 205-206
marine insurance   60, 211-213
Marine Insurance Application   212

N

O

P

R

S

T

W

Y

Z

ORDER INFORMATION

We hope you enjoyed this book! GEMINI MARINE PUBLICATIONS features practical publications of direct interest to the power boater. Developed after many years of practical experience, our material gives you what you need to know, and what you need to do.

If you want additional copies of this book, write or call us. The price is $19.95 plus $2.00 handling and postage. Shipment is by U.S. Postal Service Book Rate with delivery in about three weeks in the United States. If First Class is desired, the handling and postage charges are $3.50. Payment is welcomed by personal check, money order, or VISA/MASTERCARD. If you pay by credit card, please tell us the number, expiration date, and the name on the card.

A free catalog of our marine publications, and other unique items, may be obtained by mailing us your name and address, or by calling (210) 494-0426.

Happy Boating!

Gemini Marine Publications
16418 Ledge Trail
P.O. Box 700255-0255
San Antonio, TX 78270-0255
Telephone (210) 494-0426
Fax (210) 494-0766